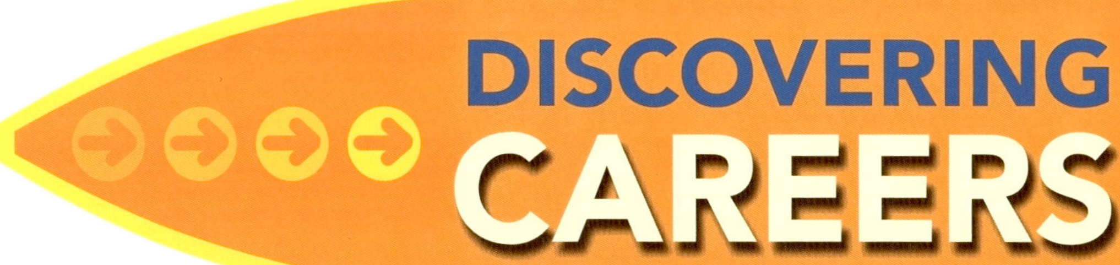

Environment

Titles in the Discovering Careers series

Adventure
Animals
Computers
Construction
Environment
Health
Math
Nature
Science
Space Exploration
Sports
Transportation

DISCOVERING CAREERS

Environment

Ferguson's

An Infobase Learning Company

Discovering Careers: Environment

Ferguson's
An imprint of Infobase Learning
132 West 31st Street
New York NY 10001

Library of Congress Cataloging-in-Publication Data

Environment.
    p. cm. — (Discovering careers series)
Includes bibliographical references and index.
ISBN-13: 978-0-8160-8050-2 (hardcover : alk. paper)
ISBN-10: 0-8160-8050-X (hardcover : alk. paper) 1. Environmental protection—
Juvenile literature.
TD170.15+.C68 2011   333.72023—dc22
 2010040591

You can find Ferguson's on the World Wide Web at
http://www.infobasepublishing.com

Text design by Erik Lindstrom and Erika K. Arroyo
Composition by Erika K. Arroyo
Cover printed by Bang Printing, Brainerd, MN
Book printed and bound by Bang Printing, Brainerd, MN
Date printed: March 2011

Printed in the United States of America

10 9 8 7 6 5 4 3 2 1

This book is printed on acid-free paper.

CONTENTS

Introduction

You may not have decided yet what you want to be in the future. And you don't have to decide right away. You do know that right now you are interested in the environment. Do any of the statements below describe you? If so, you may want to begin thinking about what a career in the environment might mean for you.

____ Environmental science is my favorite subject in school.

____ I like teaching people about nature and the environment.

____ I am concerned about preserving endangered species.

____ I love being outdoors.

____ I am interested in learning more about renewable energy.

____ I am active in recycling projects.

____ I like to study the plants and trees native to my area.

____ I am concerned about air, water, and soil pollution.

____ I participate in community clean-up projects.

____ I like to discuss environmental issues with friends and family.

____ I want to do something to help in the event of an oil spill.

____ I sign petitions and attend rallies that support protecting the environment.

____ I enjoy taking trips to state and national parks with my family.

____ I enjoy helping my family cut energy costs.

____ I like writing essays and articles about the environment.

Discovering Careers: Environment is a book about environmental careers, from air quality engineers and foresters to marine biologists and renewable energy workers. People in environment-related careers are interested in and deeply concerned about how humans interact with and change our planet. They study the earth and seek ways to reduce pollution, save land from development, utilize renewable energy resources, and conserve natural resources.

This book describes many possibilities for future careers in the environment. Read through it to see the variety of careers that are available. For example, if you are interested in animal life, you will want to read the chapters on Fish and Game Wardens, Marine Biologists, Oceanographers, and Park Rangers. If you are interested in ecology or conservation, you will want to read the chapters on Ecologists, Foresters, and Land Trust or Preserve Managers. If you are interested in business or law as it relates to the environment, you will want to read the chapters on Environmental Lawyers and Environmental Lobbyists. Perhaps you are interested in conserving energy and learning more about renewable energy resources such as wind or solar power. If so, then you should read the articles on Energy Conservation Technicians and Renewable Energy Workers. Go ahead and explore!

What Do Environmental Workers Do?

The first section of each chapter begins with a heading such as "What Environmental Engineers Do" or "What Environmental Writers Do." This section tells what it's like to work at this job. It also describes typical responsibilities and working conditions. Which environmental professionals work in forests or beneath the ocean's surface? Which ones work at computers in offices? Which work in the halls of Congress? This section answers these and other questions.

How Do I Become an Environmental Worker?

The section called "Education and Training" tells you what schooling you need for employment in each job—a high school diploma, training at a junior college, a college degree, or more. It also talks about what high school and college courses you should take to prepare for the field.

How Much Do Environmental Workers Earn?

The "Earnings" section gives the average salary figures for the job described in the chapter. These figures give you a general idea of how much money people with this job can make. Keep in mind that many people really earn more or less than the amounts given here because actual salaries depend on many different things, such as the size of the company or government agency, the location of the company, and the amount of education, training, and experience you have. Generally, but not always, larger companies located in major cities pay more than smaller ones in smaller cities and towns, and people with more education, training, and experience earn more. Also remember that these figures are current or recent averages. They will probably be different by the time you are ready to enter the workforce.

What Will the Future be Like for Environmental Workers?

The "Outlook" section discusses the employment outlook for the career: whether the total number of people employed in this career will increase or decrease in the coming years and whether jobs in this field will be easy or hard to find. These predictions are based on economic conditions, the size and makeup of the population, foreign competition, and new technology.

Keep in mind that these predictions are general statements. No one knows for sure what the future will be like. Also remember that the employment outlook is a general statement about an industry and does not necessarily apply to everyone. A determined and talented person may be able to find a job in an industry or career with the worst outlook. And a person without ambition and the proper training will find it difficult to find a job in even a booming industry or career field.

Where Can I Find More Information?

Each chapter includes a sidebar called "For More Info." It lists resources that you can contact to find out more about the field and careers in the field. You will find names, addresses, phone numbers, e-mail addresses, and Web sites of environmental associations and organizations.

Extras

Every chapter has a few extras. There are photos that show environmental workers in action. There are sidebars and notes on ways to explore the field, interesting facts, profiles of people in the field, tips on important skills for success in the field, information on work settings, lists of Web sites and books, and other resources that might be helpful.

At the end of the book you will find three additional sections: "Glossary," "Browse and Learn More," and "Index." The Glossary gives brief definitions of words that relate to education, career training, or employment that you may be unfamiliar with. The Browse and Learn More section lists environment-related books, periodicals, and Web sites to explore. The Index includes all the job titles mentioned in the book.

It's not too soon to think about your future. We hope you discover several possible career choices in the environmental field. Happy hunting!

Air Quality Engineers

What Air Quality Engineers Do

Air quality engineers develop ways to analyze and control air pollution. They help manufacturers and cities meet those federal requirements. Air quality engineers are also called *air pollution control engineers* and *environmental engineers.*

Many industrial and fuel-burning processes produce waste through exhaust or evaporation, called emissions. This is part of the cause of air pollution. For example, carbon monoxide released from automobiles and manufacturing factories is a major air pollutant.

Indoor air can become polluted, too. Poor ventilation (air flow) in a polluted building can create serious health issues for those working or living in it. This problem is known as "sick building syndrome." Air quality engineers must find the cause of the pollution in the building. Then they work to get rid of and reverse its effects on the building's inhabitants.

Air quality engineers work in several different kinds of jobs. Some air quality engineers work for manufacturers. They monitor the level of harmful pollutants in their company's emissions. They might evaluate and suggest changing parts of the industrial process that cause pollution. They also might recommend air-pollution control equipment or advise the manufacturer to use different raw materials or machinery that create less pollution.

Some engineers work as independent consultants. They advise businesses about how to limit air pollution. Other air quality engineers work for equipment manufacturers that design and sell air pollution control systems.

Some air quality engineers work for the EPA and other governmental agencies that decide how much of certain chemicals

Words to Learn

acid rain rain that contains higher than average amounts of nitric and sulfuric acids; these elements, which are generated from factories and natural events such as volcanoes, can harm the environment

carbon monoxide an odorless, colorless, poisonous gas

emissions releases of potentially harmful substances into the air, water, and soil

global warming the slow rise in our planet's average temperature caused by an increase in greenhouse gases (such as carbon dioxide, methane, and nitrous oxide); nearly all of the world's leading scientists believe that global warming is

causing major negative climate change

greenhouse effect the warming of the planet's surface as a result of manmade and natural processes; the greenhouse effect is negatively affecting our environment

ozone a highly reactive gas that can be unhealthy to humans

sulfur dioxide a colorless gas and a toxic pollutant

U.S. Environmental Protection Agency (EPA) the federal agency responsible for making sure that environmental laws are followed; these laws are designed to monitor and control air, water, and soil pollution; state EPAs help carry out these laws

are harmful to the atmosphere and to living organisms. Government air quality engineers monitor the pollution produced by businesses in their designated region. They investigate manufacturers that may be polluters and may even go to court to force manufacturers to follow the law.

Some air quality engineers research the causes and effects of specific problems such as sick building syndrome, acid rain, or the greenhouse effect. Acid rain occurs when sulfur dioxide emissions mix with moisture in the air. Sulfur dioxide is a colorless gas and a toxic pollutant that can poison wildlife and water supplies and destroy property. The greenhouse effect is the warming of the atmosphere caused by a buildup of carbon dioxide (another type of gas). These engineers committed to research and development work in public or private research institutions and in academic environments.

DID YOU KNOW?

- Nearly 62 percent of the U.S. population lives in counties that have unhealthful levels of either particle pollution or ozone (a highly reactive gas that can be unhealthy to humans).
- Fifty-eight percent of the U.S. population resides in areas with unhealthful levels of ozone.
- Approximately 40.5 million Americans live in 37 counties that have unhealthful levels of all three types of air pollutants: ozone, and short-term and year-round particle pollution.

Source: *State of the Air: 2009,* American Lung Association

Education and Training

High school classes in math, biology, and chemistry will be helpful if you are interested in becoming an air quality engineer.

You will also need a bachelor's degree in environmental or chemical engineering to work as an air quality engineer. College programs cover specific concerns of air quality engineers. These include how pollution affects health and how weather and air pollution interact. In addition, knowledge of advanced computer systems is becoming more and more important in the field of engineering.

FOR MORE INFO

For information on careers and a list of colleges and degrees offering environmental degrees, contact
Air and Waste Management Association
420 Fort Duquesne Boulevard
One Gateway Center, Third Floor
Pittsburgh, PA 15222-1435
412-232-3444
info@awma.org
http://www.awma.org

For information about careers, contact
Junior Engineering Technical Society
1420 King Street, Suite 405
Alexandria, VA 22314-2750
703-548-5387
info@jets.org
http://www.jets.org

For information about air pollution and government pollution control boards, contact
National Association of Clean Air Agencies
444 North Capitol Street, NW, Suite 307
Washington, DC 20001-1512
202-624-7864
http://www.4cleanair.org

For information about air quality and other environmental issues, contact
U.S. Environmental Protection Agency
Ariel Rios Building
1200 Pennsylvania Avenue, NW
Washington, DC 20004-2403
Tel: 202-272-0167
http://www.epa.gov

Earnings

Salaries for entry-level engineers start at around $45,000 per year. Experienced workers earn salaries that range from $74,000 to $115,000 or more.

Outlook

Air quality management has a bright future. Most people are understandably concerned about the quality of the air they breathe. As a result, the government is under much pressure to control polluted emissions. Most industries will need engineers to determine how they can control their own pollutants. As manufacturing processes develop and change, industries will need air quality engineers to monitor their new technologies.

Ecologists

What Ecologists Do

Ecologists are specialized scientists who study how plants and animals interact with and sustain each other in their environments, or habitat. An environment includes living things. It also includes nonliving elements, such as chemicals, moisture, soil, light, temperature, and things made by humans, such as buildings, highways, machines, fertilizers, and medicines. The word *ecology* is sometimes used to describe the balance of nature.

A big part of an ecologist's job is to study communities. A community is the group of organisms that share a particular habitat. For example, a *forest ecologist* might study how changes in the environment affect forests. They may study what causes a certain type of tree to grow well, including light and soil requirements, and resistance to insects and disease.

Some ecologists study biomes, which are large communities. Examples of biomes are the tropical rain forest, the prairie, the tundra, and the desert. The ocean is sometimes considered one biome.

Many ecologists study ecosystems—a living community together with its nonliving components. *Population ecologists* study why a certain population of living things increases, decreases, or remains stable.

Restoration ecologists create and implement plans to reestablish ecosystems that have been damaged by humans or natural events such as flooding.

All living things, including humans, depend on their environments to live. As a result, the work of ecologists is

EXPLORING

- Read books and other publications about ecology and the environment. You will find lots of reading material at your library or bookstore and on the Internet.
- Join a school ecology club.
- Learn more about environmental issues such as global warming, deforestation, pollution, and endangered species by contacting environmental organizations and reading books and other publications.

- Join a scouting organization or environmental protection group to gain firsthand experience in the work of an ecologist.
- Visit natural history museums to learn more about the field. Visit nearby parks or forest preserves. What kinds of trees and plants grow there? Which insects, animals, and birds are native to the area?
- Talk to an ecologist about his or her career.

extremely important in helping us understand how environments work.

Most ecologists work in land and water conservation jobs in the public sector. This includes the federal government, the largest employer of ecologists. The Bureau of Land Management, the U.S. Fish and Wildlife Service, the National Park Service, and the U.S. Geological Survey are among the federal agencies that employ ecologists. Other public sector opportunities are with regional, state, and local agencies. Opportunities in the private sector can be found with utilities, timber companies, and consulting firms. Some ecologists work as teachers at nature centers, middle schools and high schools, and colleges and universities.

Education and Training

Classes that will be useful include earth science, biology, ecology, chemistry, English, and math. Ecologists often use computers to do research and record their findings. For that reason, you should also take computer science courses.

To be an ecologist you must go to college and earn a bachelor of science degree. Recommended majors are biology, botany, chemistry, ecology, geology, physics, or zoology.

You will need a master's degree for research or management jobs. If you want to work as a college teacher or research supervisor, you will need a doctoral degree.

Tips for Success

To be a successful ecologist, you should

- love and respect nature
- know a lot about the environment
- be a good problem solver
- be able to work well with others
- have good communication skills
- be willing to work outside in all types of weather conditions

An ecologist (right) *and a technician collect samples of small organisms in a wetland.* (Peggy Greb, USDA, Agricultural Research Service)

Earnings

Salaries for ecologists vary depending on such factors as their level of education, experience, area of specialization, and the organization for which they work. Ecologists just starting out in the field might make $36,000 or less. Those with many years in the field earn $63,000 or more.

Ecological Catastrophe

Humans sometimes try to improve the environment and end up making big mistakes because they don't understand ecological balance. Ecological balance can be defined as the way in which plants and animals live together. An example of an ecological catastrophe, or disaster, occurred on Borneo (a large island in Southeast Asia) shortly after World War II (1939–1945). A program was started there to control mosquitoes by spraying DDT, an insecticide that can hurt humans and animals if swallowed or absorbed through the skin. The number of mosquitoes declined drastically, but the roofs of houses began to collapse because they were being eaten by caterpillars. The caterpillars had previously been held under control by certain predatory wasps—which had been killed off by the DDT.

In addition to spraying for mosquitoes, the villagers also sprayed inside their homes to kill flies. Previously, the houseflies had been more or less controlled by lizards called geckos. As the geckos continued eating houseflies, now laden with DDT, the geckos began to die. The dead or dying geckos were eaten by house cats. The cats also began to die from the DDT concentrated in the bodies of the geckos they were eating. So many cats died that rats began invading the houses, eating the villagers' food. The number of rats grew quickly and eventually became potential carriers of plague (a deadly disease). This example shows how careful we need to be when trying to fix an environmental problem. We have to think about what can go wrong or right during every move we make. Otherwise, disaster can happen.

FOR MORE INFO

For a wide variety of publications, including *Issues in Ecology, Careers in Ecology,* and fact sheets about specific ecological concerns, contact
Ecological Society of America
1990 M Street, NW, Suite 700
Washington, DC 20036-3415
202-833-8773
esahq@esa.org
http://esa.org

For information about internships and volunteer opportunities for teens, contact
National Wildlife Federation
11100 Wildlife Center Drive
Reston, VA 20190-5362
800-822-9919
http://www.nwf.org

Outlook

The job outlook for environmental workers in general should remain good during the next decade. But there will be fewer jobs in land and water conservation. This is because so many ecologists compete for these popular jobs. Also, many environmental organizations don't have a large amount of money available to hire ecologists.

Ecologists with advanced degrees who are willing to travel to different parts of the United States and the world will have the best job opportunities.

Energy Conservation Technicians

What Energy Conservation Technicians Do

Energy conservation technicians identify and measure the amount of energy used to heat, cool, and operate a building or industrial process. They inspect homes, businesses, or industrial buildings (such as factories) to find conditions that cause energy waste. Then they recommend ways to reduce the waste, and help install corrective measures (such as insulation on windows to reduce drafts).

Energy conservation technicians who are employed by utilities help customers reduce their utility bills. They visit customers' homes to interview them about household energy use, such as the type of heating system, the number of people home during the day, the furnace or air conditioner temperature setting, and prior heating or cooling costs. They draw a sketch of the house, measure its perimeter, windows, and doors, and record dimensions on the sketch. They inspect attics, crawl spaces, and basements and note any loose-fitting windows, uninsulated pipes, and deficient insulation (material that helps reduce energy loss). They read hot-water tank labels to find the heat-loss rating and determine the need for a tank insulation blanket. Technicians also examine air furnace filters and heat exchangers to detect dirt or soot buildup that might affect furnace operations. Once technicians identify a problem, they must know how to correct it. After discussing problems with the customer, the technician recommends repairs and provides literature on conservation improvements

A technician (left) *tests the energy efficiency of a customer's furnace.* (Robert Craig, AP Photo/*The Wilmington News-Journal*)

EXPLORING

- Read about energy conservation techniques in books and on the Internet.
- Try to reduce energy output in your daily life.
- Contact employers of energy technicians to learn about opportunities for volunteer, part-time, or summer work.
- Ask a counselor or teacher to help arrange an information interview with an energy conservation technician. Ask the following questions: What are your main and secondary job duties? What do you like least and most about your job? How did you train for this field? What advice would you give a young person who is interested in the field?

and sources of government loans (if the problem is major) that will help pay for the work.

Those in research and development often work for the military or another government agency. They design, build, and operate new laboratory experiments for physicists, chemists, or engineers. Technicians in energy production often work for power plants. They develop and operate systems for converting fuel as efficiently as possible into electricity. In the field of energy use, a technician might be hired to make heavy industrial equipment work more efficiently. After running tests and measurements, the technician usually prepares a report and discusses the results with management officials. Then technicians may make recommendations, but managers make any final decisions about what actions should be taken. A manager or supervising engineer might ask the technician to run further tests and present additional findings. After a final decision is made, technicians team up with other workers to see that any necessary corrections are made.

Education and Training

In high school, take classes such as algebra, environmental science, geometry, physics, chemistry, machine shop, ecology, computer science, and drafting.

The best way to enter this career is to complete a two-year training program at a community college or technical school. The program might be called energy conservation technology, or it may be called electric power maintenance, general engineering technology, or something similar.

DID YOU KNOW?

Where Energy Conservation Technicians Work

- Utility companies
- Large hospitals
- Office buildings
- Hotels
- Colleges and universities
- Manufacturing plants
- Government agencies

Earnings

Earnings of energy conservation technicians vary greatly based on the amount of formal training and experience they have. According to the U.S. Department of Labor, the mean annual salary for environmental engineering technicians in engineering and architectural services (a category that often includes energy conservation technicians) was $43,140 in 2008. Salaries for all environmental engineering technicians ranged from less than $26,000 to $68,000 or more annually.

Outlook

Opportunities for energy conservation technicians will be good during the next decade. Utility companies, manufacturers, and government agencies are working together to establish energy efficiency standards. They are developing programs to improve energy efficiency in commercial air-conditioning equipment, lighting, geothermal heat pumps, and other systems. Programs such as these will create job opportunities for technicians.

Conserving Energy at Home

Do the following to reduce energy output at home:

- Ask your parents to perform an energy survey or audit of your home to find ways to reduce utility bills each month.
- At home, dress appropriately (warmer clothing in the winter, cooler clothing in the summer) to help reduce heating and cooling costs.
- Turn off lights and appliances when they are not in use.
- Try to only run your dishwasher or washing machine when you have a full load ready to clean. Half-loads waste energy. Use cold water in the washing machine, when possible. Air dry dishes and laundry.
- Ask your parents to replace regular light bulbs with compact fluorescent lights, which use about one-fourth of the energy of regular light bulbs.
- Ride your bike or walk to school and other activities to save gas and reduce pollution.
- Plant deciduous (trees that lose their leaves in the fall) near your home. During the summer, the leaves will keep the sun out of your house, and in the winter, the bare trees will allow the sun in to help heat your home.
- Recycle plastics, glass, steel and aluminum cans, and newspapers.
- Purchase products that are made of recycled material.

Sources: U.S. Department of Energy, Earth911

FOR MORE INFO

For information on energy conservation, contact

Association of Energy Conservation Professionals
The Jacksonville Center
220 Parkway Lane, Box 5A
Floyd, VA 24091-4171
540-745-2838
aecp@swva.net
http://www.aecpes.org

For information on energy efficiency and renewable energy, contact

Energy Efficiency and Renewable Energy
U.S. Department of Energy
Mail Stop EE-1
Washington, DC 20585
http://www1.eere.energy.gov/education

Environmental Engineers

What Environmental Engineers Do

A waste stream can be anything from wastewater, to solid waste (garbage), to hazardous waste (such as radioactive waste), to air pollution (from a factory or other source). If a private company or a city or town does not handle its waste streams properly, it can face thousands or even millions of dollars in fines from the government for breaking the law. Most important, these waste streams can make people very sick. *Environmental engineers* play an important role in controlling waste streams.

Environmental engineers may plan a sewage system, design a manufacturing plant's emissions system (which help reduce pollution), or develop a plan for a landfill site needed to bury garbage. Scientists help decide how to break down the waste. Engineers figure out how the system will work. They decide where the pipes will go, how the waste will flow through the system, and what equipment will be needed.

Environmental engineers may work for private industrial companies, for the Environmental Protection Agency (EPA), or for engineering consulting firms.

Environmental engineers who work for private industrial companies help make sure their companies obey environmental laws. They design new waste systems or make sure the old ones are operating correctly. Engineers might, for example, plan a system to move wastewater from the manufacturing process area to a treatment area, and then to a discharge site (a place where the treated wastewater can be pumped out). Engineers might write reports explaining the design. They also might file forms with the government to prove that the company is complying with, or obeying, the laws.

Environmental engineers who work for the EPA might not design the waste treatment systems themselves, but they do have to know how such systems are designed and built. If there is a pollution problem in their area, they need to figure out if a waste control system is causing the problem, and what might have gone wrong.

Environmental engineers employed by engineering consulting firms work on many different types of problems. Consulting firms are independent companies that help others follow environmental laws. They design and build waste control systems for their clients. They also deal with the EPA on behalf of their clients. They fill out forms and check to see what requirements must be met.

EXPLORING

- Check your library, the Internet, and bookstores for reading material on engineering and the environment.
- Volunteer for the local chapter of a nonprofit environmental organization.
- Talk to an environmental engineer about his or her career.
- Contact your local EPA office, check the Yellow Pages for environmental consulting firms in your area, or ask a local industrial company if you can visit.

Education and Training

In school, take as many science and mathematics classes as possible. It's also important to develop good communication skills, so be sure to take English and speech courses.

You will have to earn a bachelor's degree to work as an environmental engineer. About 55 colleges offer a bachelor's degree in environmental engineering. Another option is to earn another type of engineering degree such as civil, industrial, or mechanical engineering, and take additional courses in environmental engineering. Some environmental engineers go on to earn graduate degrees.

Helping Hands: Yuyun Ismawati

People all around the world are doing their part to protect the environment. The work of Yuyun Ismawati is just one example of these efforts. The Indonesian environmental engineer has lived on the island of Bali since 1996. This beautiful island is a popular tourist destination for people from around the world. Ismawati noticed a major problem on the island. Tourists were generating a large amount of garbage. In fact, they were creating 10 times as much garbage as the average Indonesian creates. Hotels sold much of the waste to pig farmers. Once the pigs were done eating portions of the garbage, the rest was abandoned in natural areas around the island.

Ismawati was not happy about the littering. She knew it was ruining the environment and eventually would reduce tourism because no one would want to visit the island if it was polluted and dirty. She created BaliFokus (http://balifokus.asia/balifokus), an organization that sought to help promote waste management in local communities. Ismawati eventually convinced the hotel owners to pay to have the trash removed, sorted, and properly disposed of. Now the island is cleaner.

Ismawati was not done protecting the environment. The Indonesian government only collects 30 to 40 percent of solid waste generated by its citizens, and most of the garbage is collected in wealthy areas. The rest is discarded into big piles—especially in poor areas. The trash can be dangerous to residents. In fact, a 230-foot mountain of trash collapsed in Ismawati's hometown in 2005, killing 140 people. This incident prompted Ismawati and her organization to help create solid waste management programs in seven poor areas in Indonesia. She also encouraged the people to make traditional crafts out of some of the garbage to sell to tourists. That way, they could reduce the amount of trash and make a little money to improve their lives.

In 2008, Ismawati established the Toxics-Free Network, which sought to fight the spread of toxic substances into the environment.

In recognition of her work, Yuyun Ismawati was named a Hero of the Environment in 2009 by *Time* magazine and CNN. In that same year, she also received the Goldman Environmental Prize, a prestigious award given to those who protect the environment.

Source: Goldmanprize.org, *Time*/CNN, BaliFokus

Earnings

The U.S. Department of Labor (DOL) reports that average annual earnings of environmental engineers were $74,020 in 2008. Environmental engineers just out of college made less than $45,000. Those with a lot of experience and an advanced college degree earned $115,000 or more.

Outlook

Employment for environmental engineers will be very good in the future. Engineers will be needed to help clean up existing hazards. They will also be asked to help companies comply with government regulations. In the future, companies will ask environmental engineers to prevent problems before they happen to protect the health of the public. Jobs will be available with all three major employers—industry, the U.S. EPA and local and state EPAs, and consulting firms.

DID YOU KNOW?

Where Environmental Engineers Work

- Federal government agencies such as the Environmental Protection Agency that focus on protecting the environment
- State environmental protection agencies
- Private companies
- Engineering consulting firms
- Colleges and universities

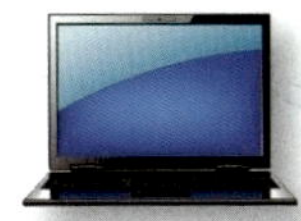

FOR MORE INFO

For information on careers, contact
American Academy of Environmental Engineers
130 Holiday Court, Suite 100
Annapolis, MD 21401-7003
410-266-3311
info@aaee.net
http://www.aaee.net

For information about environmental engineering, contact
Junior Engineering Technical Society
1420 King Street, Suite 405
Alexandria, VA 22314-2750
703-548-5387
info@jets.org
http://www.jets.org

Environmental Lawyers

What Environmental Lawyers Do

Lawyers, who are often called *attorneys,* advise people on what they can and cannot do under the law. The people lawyers help are called clients. Clients are either individuals or a group, such as a company, nonprofit organization, or government agency, or a number of people who come together because they have all been injured or wronged. *Environmental lawyers* are specialized lawyers who help government agencies and nonprofit organizations such as the Sierra Club or Greenpeace protect the environment.

Environmental lawyers who work for government agencies might be hired to take legal action against a company that is not following (or complying with) laws that protect air, land, and water from pollution. An example of this might be a manufacturing company that is releasing toxic wastewater into Lake Michigan as part of its manufacturing process. The lawyer will first contact the company via a letter to inform it that it is not in compliance with state and/or federal laws. If the company is unwilling to stop polluting or if it believes that it is not breaking the law, the environmental lawyer may have to bring the issue to court to have it resolved by a judge. Once the case is brought to court, environmental lawyers represent the government in court proceedings. They present evidence to convince the judge or jury that the company is breaking the law. A lawyer who is employed by the company will try to persuade the judge that the company did not break the law. The judge or jury eventually decides who is right in the case.

EXPLORING

- Read about environmental issues in books and magazines and on the Internet.
- Visit the Web sites of advocacy environmental organizations to learn more about important environmental causes. Here are a few suggestions: Earthwatch Institute (http://www.earthwatch.org), Friends of the Earth (http://www.foe.org), Greenpeace (http://www.greenpeace.org), National Wildlife Federation (http://www.nwf.org), The Nature Conservancy (http://nature.org), Rainforest Action Network (http://www.ran.org), Student Conservation Association (http://www.thesca.org), and The Wildlife Society (http://www.wildlife.org).
- Talk to lawyers and try to arrange to observe them working in a local courtroom or at their firms.
- Joining the speech or debate team will help you practice speaking in front of crowds and teach you how to form logical arguments.

A case may be resolved before it gets to court. The government and the company may agree to a settlement. In this instance, it is the environmental lawyer's responsibility to work with lawyers employed by the company to reach a compromise and ensure that the company does what it has promised (for example, reduce pollution emitted by its factories).

Government environmental lawyers may also play a role in land acquisition. If the government wants to acquire private land for use in a park or other nature area, the lawyer works with the landowners to purchase the land. At times, the public may not agree with the government's plans to turn an area into a park. In this instance, environmental lawyers help the government respond to lawsuits filed by people who want to stop the creation of the park.

Environmental lawyers who are employed by the Sierra Club and other nonprofit organizations fight for the protection

An environmental lawyer (left) *talks with a farmer about oil that was left behind after an oil company stopped drilling operations. The oil is damaging the farmer's crops.* (Lou Dematteis, The Image Works)

Helping Hands: Robert Kennedy Jr.

Robert Kennedy Jr. is the son of late Senator Robert Kennedy and a member of the well-known Kennedy family. The Kennedys have played a key role in American politics for more than 70 years.

Kennedy is a lawyer and an environmentalist. He serves as the chief prosecuting attorney for Riverkeeper (http://www.riverkeeper.org), an environmental organization that fights to protect and restore the Hudson River, its tributaries, and the watershed of New York City. Kennedy cites childhood outdoor adventures with his father as one of the main reasons why he loves protecting the environment.

In 1999, Kennedy founded the Waterkeeper Alliance (http://www.waterkeeper.org), which describes itself as "a global movement of on-the-water advocates who patrol and protect more than 100,000 miles of rivers, streams and coastlines in North and South America, Europe, Australia, Asia and Africa." Today, there are nearly 200 Waterkeeper Alliance organizations throughout the world.

Visit http://www.robertfkennedyjr.com to learn more about Robert Kennedy Jr. and his work to protect the environment.

Sources: Robertfkennedyjr.com, Riverkeeper.org, Waterkeeper.org

of the environment (animals, plants, entire ecosystems, human health, etc.) that are being damaged or destroyed by construction projects, pollution, energy exploration and development, and other activities. They file lawsuits against companies or government agencies that their organization believes are hurting the environment.

Education and Training

Obtaining a high school diploma is the first step to becoming an environmental lawyer. Focusing your high school studies

Tips for Success

To be a successful environmental lawyer, you should

- care deeply about protecting the environment
- have excellent communication skills, both written and oral
- be able to think on your feet
- be good at solving problems
- have strong research skills
- be very honest
- be organized
- be willing to continue to learn throughout your career

on classes such as government, political science, speech, and computer science will help prepare you for what you will study in college and law school. Courses in history, English, and environmental science will also be helpful.

A bachelor's degree is also necessary. Many environmental lawyers earn bachelor's degrees in environmental science or biology. Following college, you will study in law school for another three years. Before you can be accepted into law school, however, you must take the Law School Admission Test. Law school graduates receive either the degree of juris doctor or bachelor of laws.

All states also require law school graduates to take and pass a written exam to be admitted to the bar, or be allowed to practice law there. Because the law is constantly changing, lawyers usually continue studying throughout their careers.

Earnings

Experienced lawyers earn salaries that vary depending on the type, size, and location of their employers. The median salary for lawyers was $110,590 in 2008, according to the U.S. Department of Labor. Ten percent of lawyers earned less than $54,000. General attorneys in the federal government received average salaries of $123,660 in 2008. State government attorneys made $80,890, and local government attorneys earned $89,320.

FOR MORE INFO

For information about careers in law, contact

American Bar Association
321 North Clark Street
Chicago, IL 60654-7598
800-285-2221
askaba@abanet.org
http://www.abanet.org

For information about environmental law, contact the following organizations:

Environmental Law Alliance Worldwide
1877 Garden Avenue
Eugene, OR 97403-1927
541-687-8454
elawus@elaw.org
http://www.elaw.org

Environmental Law Institute
2000 L Street, NW, Suite 620
Washington, DC 20036-4919
202-939-3800
law@eli.org
http://www.eli.org

National Environmental Law Center
nelc@nelconline.org
http://www.nelconline.org

The FBA provides information for lawyers and judges involved in federal practice.

Federal Bar Association (FBA)
1220 North Fillmore Street, Suite 444
Arlington, VA 22201-6501
571-481-9100
fba@fedbar.org
http://fedbar.org

Outlook

Increasing numbers of legal cases involving environmental issues will create a demand for environmental lawyers. However, it is important to remember that this law specialty is small and many people want to become environmental lawyers. People with strong law school grades and a deep commitment to protecting the environment will have the best job prospects.

What Environmental Lobbyists Do

Lobbyists try to convince legislators and other public officeholders, as well as the public, to support the interests of their clients. They are hired by trade associations, labor unions, corporations, and other organizations to represent their interests in state capitals and in Washington, D.C. *Environmental lobbyists* are lobbyists who deal specifically with environmental issues. Clean air, soil, and water; global warming; genetic modification of crops; renewable energy; wildlife preservation; and conservation of natural resources are just a few of the major environmental issues brought before the government.

Environmental lobbyists try to influence legislators and government officials through both *direct* and *indirect lobbying*. Direct lobbying involves reaching legislators themselves. Environmental lobbyists meet with members of Congress, their staff members, and other members of government. They call government officials to discuss how various measures might affect the environment. They sometimes testify before congressional committees or state legislatures. They send letters and fact sheets to legislators' offices. They sometimes try to approach legislators as they travel to and from their offices. Some lobbyists ask legislators who share their views to talk about the issues with legislators who do not feel the same way. They might also try to convince members of Congress to serve as cosponsors for bills the lobbyists support. When a member of Congress becomes a cosponsor of a bill, his or her name is added to the list of members supporting that measure. Lobbyists typically assume that cosponsors will vote to support the bill. A bill's chances of one day becoming a law dramatically improve as more members agree to serve as cosponsors.

Indirect lobbying, also called *grassroots lobbying,* involves educating and motivating the public. The goal of indirect lobbying is to encourage the public to urge their representatives to vote for or against certain legislation. Environmental lobbyists use a wide variety of indirect techniques. They issue press releases about pending legislation, hoping to inspire members of the media to write topical articles. They mail letters or send e-mail or Tweets to citizens, urging them to write or call their representatives. They post information on the Internet and sometimes go door-to-door with information to mobilize members of environmental groups. On rare occasions, they take concerned citizens to state capitals or to Washington, D.C., to meet with representatives.

Lobbyists must register with government authorities and submit reports on the money they collect and spend during lobbying activities.

EXPLORING

- Read about environmental issues in books and magazines and on the Internet.
- Get involved in school government. Serve on the student council or work on student election campaigns.
- Volunteer with an environmental organization.
- Write for your school or community newspaper. Try to write stories about environmental issues affecting your school or community.
- Join the debate team or work for the school radio station to help you develop your communication and research skills.
- Ask a teacher or counselor to arrange an information interview with an environmental lobbyist.

Education and Training

Classes in speech, political science, journalism, and communications are important. You also should take biology, ecology,

DID YOU KNOW?

Lobbying has been a practice within government since colonial times. In the late 1700s, the term *lobbyist* was used to describe the special-interest representatives who gathered in the anteroom (entrance area or lobby) outside the legislative chamber in the New York state capitol. The term was sometimes a negative label. But in the 20th century, lobbyists came to be considered as experts in the fields that they represented. Members of Congress relied on them to provide information needed to evaluate legislation. During the New Deal (a series of programs created by the federal government to help reduce poverty and unemployment in the 1930s), government spending in Washington greatly increased, and the number of lobbyists grew, too.

In 1946, the Federal Regulation of Lobbying Act was passed. The act requires that anyone who spends or receives money or anything of value in the interests of passing, modifying, or defeating legislation be registered and provide spending reports. Additional regulatory acts have been passed in the years since. Most recently, the Lobbying Disclosure Act of 1995 requires all lobbyists working at the federal level to be registered.

environmental science, and chemistry in order to learn about the scientific issues behind environmental legislation.

Lobbyists have undergraduate degrees in political science, journalism, or public relations. They often hold graduate degrees in law or political science, as well. Most lobbyists enter the career after gaining a great deal of experience in another government career.

Earnings

A lobbyist's income depends on the size of the organization he or she represents. Experienced lobbyists with a solid client base can earn well over $100,000 a year. Some make more than $500,000 a year. Beginning lobbyists may earn less than $20,000 a year as they build a client base.

Outlook

As long as people continue to pollute our air, water, and soil, cut down forests, develop land, and mine the earth, environ-

Words to Learn

act a bill that has been passed by a legislature; if signed by the executive (president or governor), the bill is enacted into law

bill a written plan for a new law, which must be discussed and voted upon by a legislature

Congress the body of the U.S. government that passes laws; composed of the Senate and the House of Representatives

constituent an individual residing in an elected official's district

legislation the act of making laws

representative a member of the House of Representatives of the U.S. Congress; also referred to as a **congressperson**; representatives also serve at the state level

senator a member of the Senate of the U.S. Congress; senators also serve at the state level

veto an attempt by the executive (president or governor) to stop a bill from becoming a law

mental groups will continue to fight for legislation that will protect natural resources. Therefore, employment in this career is expected to be steady during the next decade. One thing to keep in mind is that the field is small, and it may be hard to land a full-time job as an environmental lobbyist.

FOR MORE INFO

For additional information about a career as a lobbyist, contact
American League of Lobbyists
PO Box 30005
Alexandria, VA 22310-8005

703-960-3011
alldc.org@erols.com
http://www.alldc.org

Environmental Technicians

What Environmental Technicians Do

Pollution consists of harmful things such as toxic chemicals, soot, or hazardous waste that may hurt people and the environment if not eliminated or reduced. *Environmental technicians* test water, air, and soil for contamination by pollutants. They work in laboratories and outdoors to find and control water, air, soil, and noise pollution. Most environmental technicians focus on one type of pollution. Environmental technicians are sometimes called *pollution control technicians* and *environmental science and protection technicians.*

Water pollution technicians collect samples of water from rivers, lakes, and other bodies of water or from wastewater. They perform chemical tests that show if it is contaminated, or polluted. In addition to testing the water, technicians may set up equipment to monitor water over a period of time to see if it is becoming polluted. Some technicians test water temperature, pressure (the strength and speed), flow, and other characteristics.

Air pollution technicians collect and analyze samples of gas emissions (smoke) and the atmosphere. They try to find out how badly exhaust fumes from cars and trucks are polluting the air, or whether the smoke from industrial plants contains hazardous pollution. They often set up monitoring equipment outdoors to take air samples, or they may try to create the same conditions in a laboratory.

Soil or *land pollution technicians* collect soil, silt, or mud samples so they can be checked for contamination. Soil can

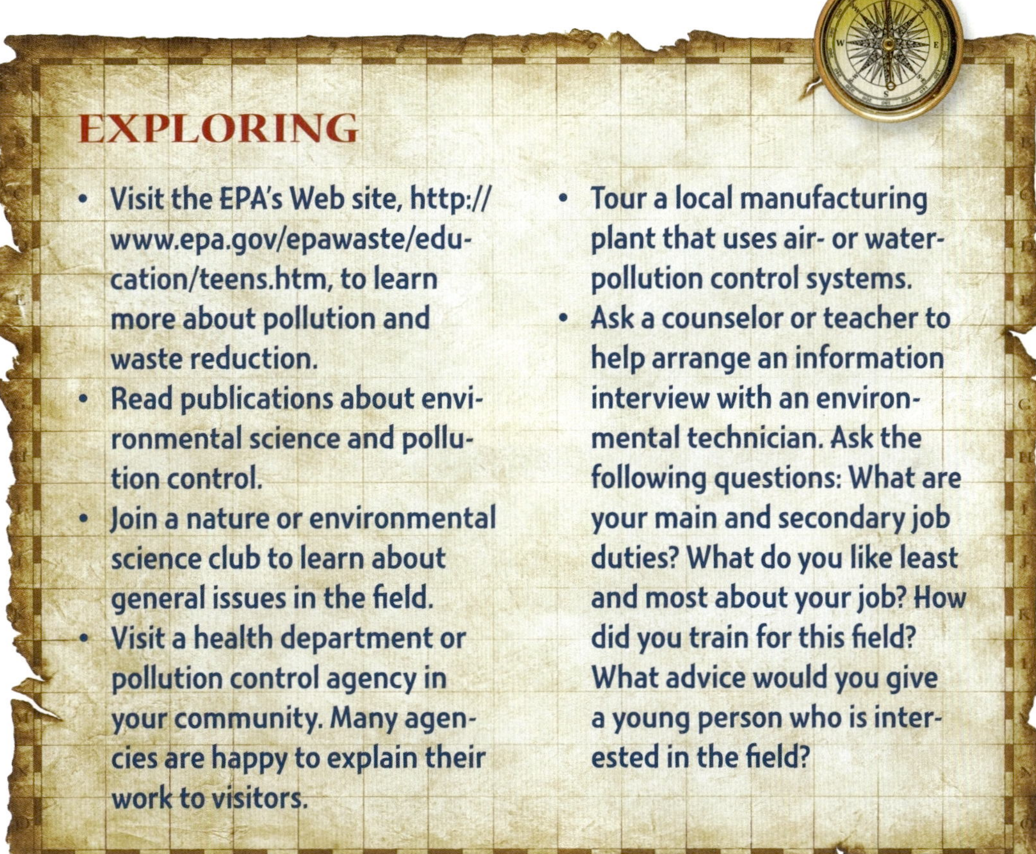

be contaminated when polluted water or waste seeps into the earth.

Some noises are so loud that they can damage people's hearing. *Noise pollution technicians* use rooftop devices and mobile units to check noise levels of factories, highways, airports, and other places. Some test noise levels of construction equipment, chain saws, lawn mowers, or other equipment. High noise levels can harm workers and the public.

Environmental technicians should be curious, patient, detail-oriented, and able to follow instructions. They need basic manual skills in order to collect samples and perform tests in laboratories. They should also be comfortable using computers and testing equipment. Environmental technicians must be

A technician (right) *and a soil scientist study a water sample.* (Scott Bauer, USDA, Agricultural Research Service)

DID YOU KNOW?

Municipal solid waste (MSW) is a major type of pollution in the United States. Solid waste is more typically known as trash or garbage. In 2008, people in the United States produced more than 250 million tons of waste. That's about 4.5 pounds of waste per person, per day! Here are the major types of MSW by percentage in 2008:

Paper: 31 percent

Yard trimmings: 13.2 percent

Food scraps: 12.7 percent

Plastics: 12 percent

Metals: 8.4 percent

Rubber, leather, and textiles: 7.9 percent

Wood: 6.6 percent

Glass: 4.9 percent

Other: 3.3 percent

All this waste really adds up year after year! Some of it pollutes our environment. But there are ways you can reduce the amount of MSW you create. Recycling, or reusing, these materials (such as paper, glass, plastic, and metals) is one good approach. These items are separated from garbage that cannot be recycled and reused as new products. Food scraps and yard trimmings can be composted in your garden. Composting involves the decomposition of these materials by microorganisms (mainly bacteria and fungi). The by-products of this decomposition help plants and trees grow.

Source: Environmental Protection Agency

able to keep accurate and detailed records. They must also be in good physical condition. They need to be willing to continue to learn throughout their careers since environmental technology is always changing.

Education and Training

Pollution control is highly technical work. You will need to take as many mathematics (algebra and geometry) and laboratory science (chemistry, physics, and biology) courses as you can in high school. Communications, computer science, conservation, and ecology classes are also important.

DID YOU KNOW?

Where Water Pollution Technicians Work

- Manufacturers that produce wastewater
- Government agencies such as the EPA and the U.S. Departments of Agriculture, Energy, and Interior
- Municipal wastewater treatment facilities
- Private firms that monitor or control pollutants in water or wastewater

After high school, you need to complete a two-year program in environmental technology. These programs are offered at community and junior colleges, and at technical schools. Some employers also offer on-the-job training for new employees.

Earnings

Pay for environmental technicians varies widely depending on the nature of the work they do, training and experience required for the work, type of employer, geographic region, and other factors.

According to the U.S. Department of Labor, the average annual salary for environmental science and protection technicians was $40,230 in 2008. Salaries ranged from less than $25,000 (new workers) to more than $65,000 (experienced workers). Technicians who worked for local and state governments earned average salaries of about $47,000 in 2008. Environmental technicians employed by colleges and universities earned about $43,000. Technicians who become managers or supervisors can earn $70,000 per year or more. Technicians who work in private industry or who further their education in order to become teachers can also expect to earn higher-than-average salaries.

Outlook

There should be many new jobs for environmental technicians in the future. They will be needed to collect soil, water, and air samples to measure pollution levels. There will also be many positions available for technicians to clean up contaminated sites and make sure that private companies follow envi-

FOR MORE INFO

For information about environmental careers and degree programs, contact
Advanced Technology Environmental and Energy Center
500 Belmont Road
Bettendorf, IA 52722-5649
http://www.ateec.org

For information about careers and a list of colleges that offer environmental degrees, contact
Air and Waste Management Association
420 Fort Duquesne Boulevard
One Gateway Center, Third Floor
Pittsburgh, PA 15222-1435
412-232-3444
info@awma.org
http://www.awma.org

For industry information, contact
National Ground Water Association
601 Dempsey Road
Westerville, OH 43081-8978

800-551-7379
ngwa@ngwa.org
http://www.ngwa.org

For information about environmental careers, resources and activities for young people, and volunteer opportunities for high school students, contact
U.S. Environmental Protection Agency
Ariel Rios Building
1200 Pennsylvania Avenue, NW
Washington, DC 20004-2403
202-272-0167
http://www.epa.gov/kids

For information about water and sanitation, contact
Water Environment Federation
601 Wythe Street
Alexandria, VA 22314-1994
800-666-0206
http://www.wef.org

ronmental laws. The demand for environmental technicians should continue due to public concern for the environment.

There will be jobs available wherever there are a lot of factories and strict state and local pollution control laws. As long as the federal government supports pollution control, the environmental control industry will continue to grow.

Environmental Writers

What Environmental Writers Do

Writers express their ideas in words for books, magazines, newspapers, advertisements, radio, television, films, and the Internet. Writers' jobs are a combination of creativity and hard work. *Environmental writers,* as you might have guessed, specialize in writing about the environment. They write about every environmental-related topic imaginable—from the daily habits of buffalo and bears, to recommended wildflower viewing areas in state and national parks, to ecofriendly vacation destinations, to serious issues that affect the environment such as deforestation, pollution, global warming, suburban sprawl, and threats to endangered species. Other environmental writers create scripts about nature and environmental issues for television and film documentaries.

Good environmental writers gather as much information as possible about a subject and then carefully check the accuracy of their sources. This can involve extensive library research, interviews, and long hours of observation and personal experience at state and national parks, in laboratories, and at sites that are polluted. Writers keep notes from which they prepare an outline or summary. They write a first draft and then rewrite sections of the material, always searching for the best way to express an idea or opinion. A manuscript is reviewed, corrected, and revised many times before a final copy is ready.

Environmental writers work for newspaper, periodical, book, and directory publishers; radio and television broadcasting companies, and nonprofit organizations such as the Sierra Club

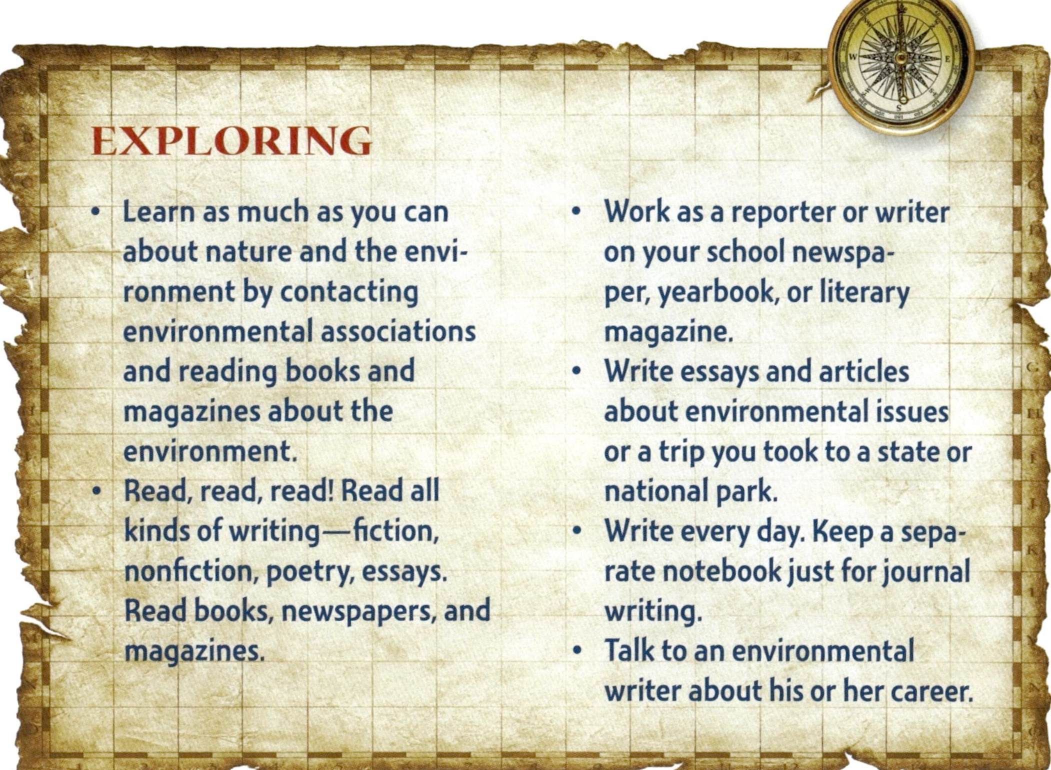

that seek to protect the environment. They also work as creative writing teachers at colleges and universities. Many writers are self-employed. They sell articles and books they write to newspaper, magazine, and book publishers.

Education and Training

In high school, take courses in English, literature, foreign languages, history, general science, environmental science, biology, social studies, computer science, and typing.

A college education is usually necessary if you want to become an environmental writer. You should also know how to use a computer for word processing and be able to handle the pressure of deadlines. Some employers prefer to hire people who have a communications or journalism degree. Others require majors in English, literature, history, philosophy, or one of the

Tips for Success

To be a successful environmental writer, you should

- care deeply about the environment
- be creative
- have excellent writing skills
- be a good researcher
- have a curious personality
- have a good memory
- be able to work under deadline pressure

social sciences. Other environmental writers have degrees in environmental-related majors such as biology, environmental science, environmental engineering, or oceanography.

Some environmental writers learn their skills on their own. A few become successful without a college education, but most have attended at least some college-level courses.

Earnings

Salaries for all writers ranged from less than $28,000 to more than $106,000 in 2008, according to the U.S. Department of Labor. Writers employed by the newspaper, book, and directory publishing industries earned average salaries of about $52,000. Best-selling authors may make well over $200,000 per year, but they are few in number.

Many creative writers work at other jobs and pursue creative writing on a part-time basis. Some authors get grants to allow them to do their writing. Others win prizes and awards.

Outlook

Employment opportunities in writing are expected to be good over the next decade. Jobs should be available at newspapers, magazines, book publishers, advertising agencies, businesses, media companies, and nonprofit organizations. However, competition for jobs is very intense.

There are many environmental-related topics to write about. But it is important to keep in mind that only a small number

Helping Hands: Don Henley and The Walden Woods Project

Henry David Thoreau (1817–1862) was an American author and naturalist. His *Walden* (1854) is a classic of American literature. It tells about the two years he lived in a small cabin on the shore of Walden Pond near Concord, Massachusetts. In *Walden,* Thoreau describes the changing seasons and other natural events and scenes that he observed in what became known as Walden Woods.

Because of Thoreau's writings, Walden Woods became a treasured place. Approximately 60 percent of the area was protected from development. But in the mid-1980s, developers decided to build condominiums and an office building on some of the unprotected areas. People were upset that these beautiful natural areas would be destroyed, but they did not have the money or power to stop the development. They feared that construction would begin.

Don Henley, an environmentalist and a member of the well-known rock group the Eagles, was also upset that the land was going to be developed. In 1990, he founded the Walden Woods Project to save the land from development. He used his fame and wealth to fund efforts to stop construction. He told everyone he could about what was happening to the land. People began to donate money to the fight and the news media began to cover the story. Within a few years, the land was purchased and saved from development.

Today, the majority of Walden Woods is protected from development. Nature-lovers from around the world visit Walden Woods to experience the natural world described in *Walden.*

Henley continues to use his wealth and fame to help protect natural wonders and educate people about environmental issues such as protecting wetlands and endangered species and improving the quality of our air and water.

Visit http://www.mass.gov/dcr/parks /walden to learn more about Walden Woods.

Source: The Walden Woods Project, http://www.walden.org

FOR MORE INFO

For information about careers, contact
National Association of Science Writers
PO Box 7905
Berkeley, CA 94707-0905
510-647-9500
http://www.nasw.org

For information on editorial writing, contact
National Conference of Editorial Writers
3899 North Front Street
Harrisburg, PA 17110-1583
717-703-3015
ncew@pa-news.org
http://www.ncew.org

For information about working as a writer and union membership, contact
National Writers Union
256 West 38th Street, Suite 703
New York, NY 10018-9807
212-254-0279
http://www.nwu.org

For information on contests for students in grades six through 12, contact
Outdoor Writers Association of America
121 Hickory Street, Suite 1
Missoula, MT 59801-1896
406-728-7434
http://owaa.org

For information on journalism, contact
Society of Professional Journalists
Eugene S. Pulliam National Journalism Center
3909 North Meridian Street
Indianapolis, IN 46208-4011
317-927-8000
http://www.spj.org

of writers specialize in writing about the environment. Many write about a wide range of topics as part of their job duties. Writers with knowledge of many fields—not just the environment—will have the best job prospects.

Fish and Game Wardens

What Fish and Game Wardens Do

Fish and game wardens protect wildlife and manage natural resources. They also teach the public and make sure that environmental laws are followed. Fish and game wardens are also called *wildlife conservationists, wildlife inspectors, refuge rangers, refuse managers,* and *refuge officers.* They are employed at the local, state, and federal levels.

The conservation, or protection, of fish and wildlife is a task that grows more complex each year. Increasing pollution and changes in the environment are putting many animals at risk. To accomplish its mission, the U.S. Fish and Wildlife Service, for example, employs many of the country's best biologists, wildlife managers, engineers, and law enforcement agents. These professionals work to save endangered and threatened species and conserve migratory birds and inland fisheries. They also provide expert advice to other federal agencies, state and local agencies, industry, and foreign governments and manage more than 700 offices and field stations. These personnel work in every state and territory—from the Arctic Ocean to the South Pacific, and from the Atlantic to the Caribbean.

Wildlife inspectors and *special agents* are two jobs that fall in the fish and game warden category of the U.S. Fish and Wildlife Service. Wildlife inspectors monitor the legal trade of federally protected fish and wildlife. They also intercept, or stop, illegal imports and exports. Some animals are so rare that it is against the law to hunt them or bring them into (import) or take them out of (export) the United States.

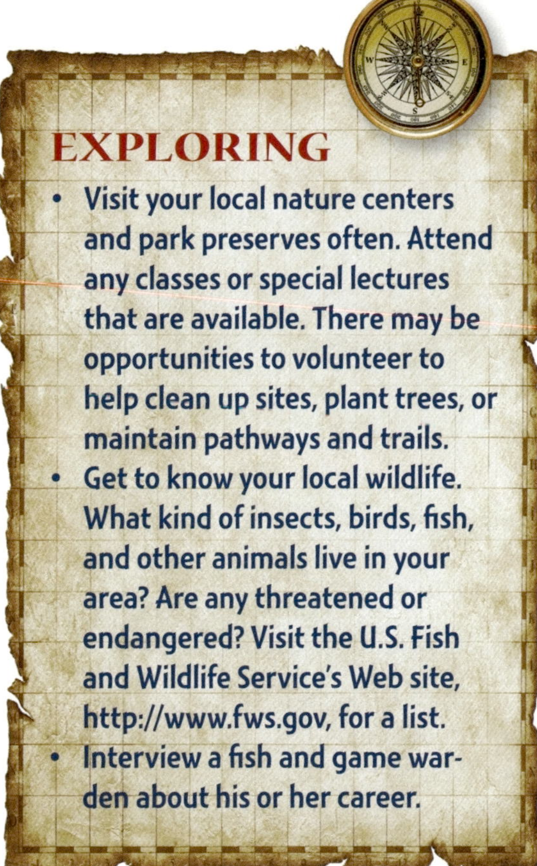

EXPLORING

- Visit your local nature centers and park preserves often. Attend any classes or special lectures that are available. There may be opportunities to volunteer to help clean up sites, plant trees, or maintain pathways and trails.
- Get to know your local wildlife. What kind of insects, birds, fish, and other animals live in your area? Are any threatened or endangered? Visit the U.S. Fish and Wildlife Service's Web site, http://www.fws.gov, for a list.
- Interview a fish and game warden about his or her career.

At points of entry into the United States, wildlife inspectors examine shipping containers, live animals, wildlife products such as animal skins, and documents. Inspectors, who work closely with special agents, may seize shipments as evidence, conduct investigations, and testify in courts of law.

Special agents of the U.S. Fish and Wildlife Service are trained criminal investigators who enforce federal wildlife laws throughout the country. Special agents conduct investigations. These may involve surveillance (observing people to see if they are breaking the law), undercover work, making arrests, and preparing cases for court. These agents enforce migratory bird regulations (laws that protect birds when they travel from one place to another) and investigate illegal trade in protected wildlife.

Refuge rangers or refuge managers work at 550 national refuges across the country. They help protect and conserve migratory and native species of birds, mammals, fish, endangered species, and other wildlife. Many of these refuges also offer outdoor recreational opportunities and educational programs.

Education and Training

Courses in biology and other sciences, geography, mathematics, social studies, and physical education will help you prepare for this career.

To become a fish and game warden, you must have a bachelor's degree or three years of work experience. Higher positions require at least one year of graduate studies. Some professional positions, such as biologist or manager, require master's or doctoral degrees.

On-the-job training is given for most positions. Special agents receive 18 weeks of formal training in criminal investigation and wildlife law enforcement techniques at the Federal Law Enforcement Training Center in Glynco, Georgia.

Fish and game wardens should be in good physical shape since they spend a lot of time outdoors in sometimes rugged conditions monitoring and protecting wildlife. To qualify for a special agent position, they must meet strict medical, physical, and psychological requirements. They must also participate in mandatory drug testing and psychological screening programs.

It is important to keep in mind that fish and game wardens don't just work with fish and game. They spend a lot of time working with other conservation professionals and with the general public. Therefore, they must have good communication skills and enjoy working with people as much as animals.

DID YOU KNOW?

Endangered species are those that have so few individual survivors that they may become extinct. At least 1,320 plants and animals in the United States alone currently are endangered, according to the U.S. Fish and Wildlife Service. Visit http://www.fws.gov/endangered to learn more about endangered species and what the U.S. Fish and Wildlife Service is doing to protect these plants and animals.

Earnings

In the wide variety of positions available at the U.S. Fish and Wildlife Service, salaries range from $21,000 for new workers up to $149,000 for more advanced positions. Law enforcement workers, especially special agents, receive higher salaries than support workers because their jobs are more dangerous.

Outlook

There will always be a need for fish and game wardens to protect natural resources. The largest number of jobs in the field are

Tips for Success

To be a successful fish and game warden, you should

- be in good physical condition
- ejoy being outdoors
- wnt to help protect the environment
- be willing to travel for job assignments
- have good communication skills
- be firm when dealing with law breakers

with the U.S. Fish and Wildlife Service and the National Park Service. State agencies, such as departments of natural resources or departments of parks and recreation, also offer jobs.

Employment growth in this field depends on politics and government. Some presidents and governors spend more on wildlife concerns, while others make cutbacks in this area. When funding is available, there are more opportunities for fish and game wardens.

FOR MORE INFO

You can learn more about fish and game wardens and related employment opportunities by contacting the following organizations:

National Park Service
U.S. Department of the Interior
1849 C Street, NW
Washington, DC 20240-0001

202-208-6843
http://www.nps.gov

U.S. Fish and Wildlife Service
U.S. Department of the Interior
4401 North Fairfax Drive
Arlington, VA 22203-1610
800-344-WILD
http://www.fws.gov

Foresters

What Foresters Do

The United States has the fourth largest amount of forested land of all the countries in the world. Its forests are beautiful and diverse. They feature many types of plants and trees. Many animals live in them. People enjoy hiking, camping, and nature watching in forests. *Foresters* protect and manage our forests. They plant trees, control diseases or insects, scatter seeds, and prune, or cut, trees. They map the locations of resources, such as places animals rest, food, snow, and water. Some foresters create the plans for building campgrounds and shelters, supervise work crews, and inspect the work after it is done.

Fires often damage or destroy forests. To help prevent forest fires, foresters select and mark dead or diseased trees to be cut. They may also use a controlled burn: When a large amount of dead plants and trees build up on the forest floor, there is a major risk that a fire could start and destroy the forest and even threaten the lives of people who live nearby. A controlled burn is a planned low-intensity fire that is set by professionals to reduce the chance of a larger fire destroying the forest. Foresters are also in charge of the lookouts, patrols, and pilots who watch for fires. They also lead crews that fight fires. Some foresters supervise campgrounds, find lost hikers, and rescue climbers and skiers. Foresters must record the work done in the forest on maps and in reports. Sometimes they use computers and data processing equipment. They also use aerial photography. Some do research in laboratories, greenhouses, and forests.

EXPLORING

- Read about trees and forests. Learn the names and types of trees and plants in forests.
- Visit the Web sites of colleges and universities that offer programs in forestry. Visit http://www.safnet.org for a list of programs.
- Visit forest preserves in your area.
- In some parts of the country, local chapters of the Society of American Foresters (http://www.safnet.org) invite students who are interested in forestry to some of their meetings and field trips.
- Talk with someone already working as a forester or forestry technician. Your science teacher or counselor may be able to help you set up a meeting.
- Plant a tree! Visit the following Web sites for more information: American Forests: How to Plant a Tree (http://www.americanforests.org/plant-trees/howto.php), How to Plant a Tree (http://www.ehow.com/how_2379114_plant-tree.html), and TreeHelp.com: How to Plant a Tree (http://www.treehelp.com/howto/howto-plant-a-tree.asp).

Foresters may specialize. For example, *silviculturists* specialize in the establishment and reproduction of forests. They regulate the types and numbers of trees and plants that are in a forest, and they manage forest growth and development. *Forest ecologists* study how forests are affected by changes in environmental conditions, such as light, soil, climate, altitude, and animals. *Urban foresters* live and work in urban areas. They oversee trees and related ecosystems (a group of organisms living together with nonliving components) in forests and woodlands, as well as those on city streets. *Conservation education foresters* teach students and educators about the proper care and management of forests.

A forester (center) *teaches high school students how to plant a tree.* (Bob Linder, AP Photo/*The Springfield News-Leader*)

Education and Training

To prepare for this field, take as many math and science courses as possible in school. Take algebra, geometry, and statistics as well as biology, chemistry, physics, and any science courses that will teach you about ecology and forestry. English classes are also important to take since part of your job is likely to include research, writing reports, and presenting your findings. In addition, take history, economics, and, if possible, agriculture classes, which will teach you about soils and plant growth, among other things.

DID YOU KNOW?

- There are approximately 755 million acres of forestland in the United States.
- Twenty percent of these forests are protected by conservation programs.
- Forty-three percent of U.S. forests are owned by state and federal agencies.

Source: *The State of America's Forests*

DID YOU KNOW?

Where Foresters Work

- Federal government agencies such as the Forest Service, the Bureau of Land Management, and the National Park Service
- State and local agencies
- Private companies (logging and lumber companies, sawmills, and research and testing facilities)
- Self-employment

A professional forester must graduate from a four-year school of forestry with a bachelor's degree. Some foresters have master's degrees. Most schools of forestry are part of state universities. In forestry school, you learn how to manage forests and make them healthy. You work in the forest as a part of your university training.

Earnings

In 2006, most bachelor's degree graduates entering the federal government as foresters earned $28,862 or $35,752, depending on their grades in school, according to the U.S. Department of Labor (DOL). Those with a master's degree started at $43,731 or $52,912, and those with doctorates started at $63,417.

Median annual earnings of foresters were $53,570 in 2008, according to the DOL. New foresters earned less than $35,000. Very experienced workers made more than $78,000 a year. In 2008, foresters working for the federal government earned an average salary of $66,670.

Outlook

Job opportunities in forestry are expected to grow more slowly than the average for all careers. Budget cuts in federal programs have limited hiring. Also, federal land management agencies, such as the U.S. Forest Service, are giving less attention to timber programs and

FOR MORE INFO

For information on forestry and forests in the United States, contact
American Forests
PO Box 2000
Washington, DC 20013-2000
202-737-1944
info@amfor.org
http://www.americanforests.org

For information about forests, forestry careers, and schools, contact
Society of American Foresters
5400 Grosvenor Lane
Bethesda, MD 20814-2198
866-897-8720
safweb@safnet.org
http://www.safnet.org

For information about urban forestry, contact
Society of Municipal Arborists
http://www.urban-forestry.com

For information about government careers in forestry and national forests across the country, contact
U.S. Forest Service
U.S. Department of Agriculture
Attn: Office of Communication
Mailstop: 1111
1400 Independence Avenue, SW
Washington, DC 20250-1111
800-832-1355
info@fs.fed.us
http://www.fs.fed.us

are focusing more on law enforcement, wildlife management, recreation, stopping wildfires, and taking care of ecosystems. This development is good for environmental workers in general, but may create fewer jobs for foresters and more openings for people in other environmental careers. Overall, there will be more opportunities at the federal and state levels than at the local level.

What Groundwater Professionals Do

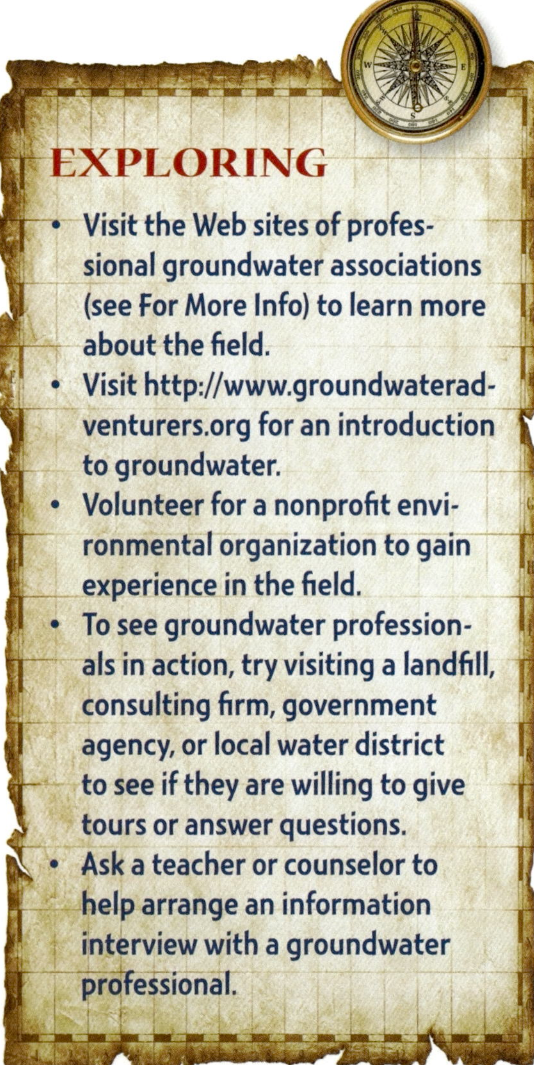

EXPLORING

- Visit the Web sites of professional groundwater associations (see For More Info) to learn more about the field.
- Visit http://www.groundwateradventurers.org for an introduction to groundwater.
- Volunteer for a nonprofit environmental organization to gain experience in the field.
- To see groundwater professionals in action, try visiting a landfill, consulting firm, government agency, or local water district to see if they are willing to give tours or answer questions.
- Ask a teacher or counselor to help arrange an information interview with a groundwater professional.

In addition to the water you see at the surface of the earth, such as lakes, streams, rivers, ponds, canals, and oceans, there is water under the ground, known as groundwater. *Groundwater professionals* monitor groundwater quality, map groundwater supplies, and find ways to clean up contaminated groundwater (water that is unfit to drink). They also find new sources of quality groundwater, bring it to the surface, and make sure that it is managed properly.

Groundwater professionals include all scientists and other workers concerned with groundwater. For example, some *geologists* help a local water district locate a new source of groundwater. *Civil engineers* design the wells and pumps needed to get the water to the surface. *Chemists* test the water to make sure it is safe to drink. *Hydrologists* study underground and surface water and its prop-

DID YOU KNOW?

- There are nearly 170,000 public water systems in the United States.
- People can only live about five to seven days without water.
- The average person should consume 2.5 quarts of water per day (via drinking and food sources).
- Freshwater makes up only 2.5 percent of all water on the earth. Most of this water is frozen at the earth's poles.
- More than 1.1 billion people worldwide do not have access to a safe and adequate water supply.

Sources: Environmental Protection Agency, WaterPartners International, American Water Works Association

erties, including how water is distributed and how it moves through land. Groundwater professionals use the scientific principles of geology, chemistry, mathematics, engineering, and physics in their work.

Some groundwater professionals gather information on the quality of water to ensure that it is safe to use. They test water samples for signs of pollution. They must be aware of chemicals or garbage that could drain into the water supply from a waste disposal site or other location.

Some groundwater professionals spend time in the field testing water and conducting other research. They work outdoors in all types of weather and may spend a great deal of time traveling from site to site.

Tips for Success

To be a successful groundwater professional, you should

- be curious and able to solve complex problems
- have good communication skills
- be attentive to detail
- be able to work as part of a team
- have an understanding of governmental rules and regulations concerning groundwater

Employers of groundwater professionals include local water districts, government agencies, consulting firms, landfill operations, private industry, and others with an interest in studying and managing groundwater. Some groundwater professionals are employed as teachers at colleges and universities.

Education and Training

To become a groundwater professional, take a lot of classes in math and science, particularly the physical and earth sciences. Technology is important in this field, so make sure you have computer skills.

You will need to earn a bachelor's degree to work as a groundwater professional. Geology, civil engineering, or chemistry are common undergraduate majors in this field. Engineering, geology (the study of rocks and minerals), hydrogeology (the science of groundwater supplies), hydrology (the study of water and its properties), geophysics (the study of matter and energy and how they interact), mining technology, engineering, or other related degrees also are useful.

Many people in this field also have a master's or a doctoral degree. Course work should include classes in water chemistry, physics, groundwater science, fluid mechanics, and calculus. Classes in computer science also are helpful.

Earnings

Earnings for groundwater professionals vary greatly depending on the type of work they do, training and experience required for the work, geographic region, type of employer, and other factors.

The U.S. Department of Labor reports that hydrologists earned median annual salaries of $71,450 in 2008. Those just starting out in the field earned less than $44,000. Very experienced workers earned more than $105,000.

A groundwater professional collects water samples taken from a river. (David Jennings, The Image Works)

FOR MORE INFO

For information about careers in the geosciences, contact

American Geological Institute
4220 King Street
Alexandria, VA 22302-1502
703-379-2480
http://www.agiweb.org

For information about certification and related organizations, contact

American Institute of Hydrology
Southern Illinois University-Carbondale
Engineering D, Mail Code 6603,
1230 Lincoln Drive
Carbondale, IL 62901
618-453-7809
aih@engr.siu.edu
http://www.aihydrology.org

For information about water quality and supply, contact

American Water Works Association
6666 West Quincy Avenue
Denver, CO 80235-3098
800-926-7337
http://www.awwa.org

For industry information, contact

National Ground Water Association
601 Dempsey Road
Westerville, OH 43081-8978
800-551-7379
ngwa@ngwa.org
http://www.ngwa.org

Outlook

Employment for hydrologists and environmental scientists will be excellent during the next decade. The continued growth of our nation's population makes finding and correcting groundwater supplies an even more important issue. Private industry needs to obey stricter rules (known as regulations), including those related to keeping groundwater safe from contamination. Local, regional, and state government agencies need to map, develop, and protect their groundwater supplies. Consultants need the specific skill that groundwater professionals can offer, for clients both in the United States and abroad. Research is needed to develop new ways to treat contaminated groundwater, to prevent spills or leaks, and to develop systems that will make the most of groundwater supplies. All of this means that employment for groundwater professionals will be excellent in the near future.

Hazardous Waste Management Specialists

What Hazardous Waste Management Specialists Do

Hazardous materials are defined by the Environmental Protection Agency (EPA) as those harmful to the environment or health. They can make us very sick or even cause death in extreme cases. *Hazardous waste management specialists* are part of a team that identifies waste sites and remediates, or cleans up, waste.

The title hazardous waste management specialist covers a group of people who prevent spills or contamination before they happen, help to control them when they do, identify contaminated sites that have existed for years, and clean up and dispose of hazardous waste.

When a polluted site is identified, specialists study the site and determine what hazardous substances are involved. Then they find out how bad the damage is and what can be done to remove the waste and restore the site. They suggest ways to do the cleanup within legal, economic, and other constraints. Once the cleanup is underway, teams of specialists make sure the waste is removed and the site properly restored. Some specialists supervise *hazardous waste management technicians* who do the sampling, monitoring, and testing at suspect sites.

Not all of the hazardous waste management specialist's time is spent in the field or in the lab. Because management of

EXPLORING

- Visit http://www.epa.gov/glossary for a glossary of hazardous waste management terms.
- Read magazines and other publications about hazardous waste management. Two suggestions: the *Journal of Environmental Quality* (https://www.agronomy.org/publications/jeq) and the *Journal of Environmental Health* (http://www.neha.org/JEH). Although these publications are for practicing environmental protection professionals, scanning the publications will give you an idea of the issues faced by workers in the field.
- Get involved in local chapters of citizen watchdog groups and become familiar with nearby Superfund (http://www.epa.gov/superfund) sites. Ask the following questions: What is being done at those sites? Who is responsible for the cleanup? What effect does the site have on its community?
- Ask your science teacher to set up an information interview with a hazardous waste management specialist. Ask the following questions: What made you want to become a hazardous waste management specialist? What do you like most and least about your job? How did you train for this field? What type of safety measures do you take on the job? What advice would you give to someone interested in the career?

hazardous waste is highly regulated (governed by law), specialists must complete a large amount of record-keeping and paperwork.

Many hazardous waste management specialists are employed by federal, state, and local governments. Others work in the private sector for companies as salaried employees or consultants. Some specialists are employed by citizen groups and environmental organizations.

To be a successful hazardous waste management specialist, you should be willing to work with toxic materials, have technical and scientific aptitude, and be able to think quickly on your feet. You should also be able to work as a member of a team and have good communication skills. A willingness to continue to learn throughout your career will help keep you up to date regarding technological developments in the field.

Education and Training

Students interested in a career in hazardous waste management should concentrate on science courses, especially chemistry, biology, and geology. Computer science, mathematics, speech, and communications courses will also be helpful.

Words to Learn

abatement reducing the amount of, or eliminating, pollution

bioremediation the use of small microorganisms to consume contamination

Comprehensive Environmental Response, Compensation, and Liability Act (CERCLA) 1980 law (known as "Superfund") that mandated cleanup of private and government-owned hazardous waste sites

contamination the introduction of a harmful substance (such as chemicals, toxic substances, or wastewater) into air, soil, or water

groundwater water located beneath the surface of the earth

National Priorities List U.S. EPA list of the worst hazardous waste sites in the country needing cleanup

sampling taking quantities of water, soil, or air from a site; samples are tested in labs to check for the presence of hazardous substances

toxicity degree to which a chemical or other substance is harmful to health or the environment

Americans produce 1.6 million tons of household hazardous waste per year, according to the EPA. The average home stores as much as 100 pounds of household hazardous waste in its basement, garage, and closets.

Products containing hazardous ingredients may include paints, cleaners, stains and varnishes, car batteries, motor oil, and pesticides. The used or left-over portions of these products is known as household hazardous waste. Sometimes people dispose of this waste improperly. They may pour it down the drain, on the ground, into storm sewers, or throw it in the trash. All of these practices can be dangerous. Instead, follow instructions on the label for proper disposal or take household hazardous waste to a proper collection facility.

Although some specialists enter this field with undergraduate degrees in engineering—environmental, chemical, or civil—it is not strictly necessary for the work involved. Many employers in this field train their employees with the help of technical institutes or community colleges with courses on hazardous waste disposal. A bachelor's degree in environmental resource management, chemistry, geology, or ecology also may be acceptable. Areas of expertise such as hydrology or subsurface hydrology may require a master's or doctoral degree.

Earnings

The U.S. Department of Labor reports that median earnings of hazardous materials removal workers were $37,310 in 2008. Salaries ranged from less than $23,000 to more than $63,000 annually.

Hazardous waste workers employed by the private sector have middle-range salaries of $40,000 to $50,000 per year. Specialists with degrees in areas of high demand, such as toxicology or hydrology, can earn $80,000 or more, depending on seniority and certification levels.

Outlook

There is no shortage of contaminated sites in the United States. Specialist jobs are fairly secure, but the hazardous waste management industry continues to change. The cleanup of sites is usually very costly, and sites can only be cleaned if government

FOR MORE INFO

For information about hazardous waste management training and degree programs, contact
Advanced Technology Environmental Education Center
500 Belmont Road
Bettendorf, IA 52722-5649
http://www.ateec.org

For information about certification, contact the following organizations:
Institute of Hazardous Materials Management
11900 Parklawn Drive, Suite 450
Rockville, MD 20852-2624
301-984-8969
info@ihmm.org
http://www.ihmm.org

National Environmental Health Association
720 South Colorado Boulevard,
Suite 1000-N
Denver, CO 80246-1926
303-756-9090
staff@neha.org
http://www.neha.org

For information on hazardous waste management training and degree programs nationwide, contact
Partnership for Environmental Technology in Education
natlpete@maine.rr.com
http://www.nationalpete.org

The Army Corps of Engineers is a sub-branch of the military that employs engineering professionals in hazardous waste management projects such as Superfund remediation sites.
U.S. Army Corps of Engineers
441 G Street, NW
Washington, DC 20314-1000
202-761-0011
hq-publicaffairs@usace.army.mil
http://www.usace.army.mil

funding is available. Public pressure to clean up sites has kept environmental funding steady over the years, though. Industry experts predict that future job markets will focus more on waste prevention, as opposed to waste removal, treatment, and disposal.

Land Trust or Preserve Managers

What Land Trust or Preserve Managers Do

Land that is especially beautiful, has rare plants or animals living on it, or is special in other ways is often kept from being developed (or built up), polluted, mined, too heavily farmed, or otherwise damaged. This type of protection is called a land trust or preserve. Hundreds of millions of acres of land and water are protected in this way. Land trusts and preserves are owned by private organizations, preserves, and the government.

Land trust and preserve managers plan for recreational use of land and water, such as hiking or camping. They count the plant and animal species and protect wildlife habitats. They clean up pollution. They restore damaged ecosystems. They manage forests, prairies, rangelands, and wetlands using techniques such as controlled burnings and grazing by bison or cattle.

Land trust managers work for private, nonprofit land trusts. Land trusts have become an important way for people who care about the environment to take action. For example, in the 1970s, a land trust saved miles of San Francisco coastline from development (the building of roads, buildings, and other structures). Land trusts get land by buying it, accepting it as a donation, or purchasing the development rights to it. Land trusts can be small; one person might do everything. A few land trusts have a large, paid staff of 30 or more.

Preserve managers work for the federal government, which owns more than 700 million acres, about one-third of the United States. This land includes forests, wilderness areas, wildlife refuges, scenic rivers, and other sites. Most of this land is managed by agencies, such as the National Park Service, U.S. Fish and Wildlife Service, Bureau of Land Management, and U.S. Forest Service. State and local governments also may own and

Profile: Teddy Roosevelt

One of the most important people in early conservation efforts was Theodore Roosevelt. He was the 26th president of the United States. Roosevelt fell in love with the West (areas that are west of the Mississippi River) as a young man, when illness led him there to seek better air. He owned a ranch in the Dakota Territory (what is now North and South Dakota) and wrote many books about his experiences in the West.

When he became president in 1901, Roosevelt used his influence to help preserve his beloved West. He promoted conservation as part of an overall strategy for the responsible use of natural resources, including forests, pastures, fish, game, soil, and minerals. His efforts increased public awareness of and support for conservation. They also led to important early conservation legislation. Roosevelt's administration especially emphasized the preservation of forests, wildlife, park lands, wilderness areas, and watershed areas and carried out such work as the first inventory of natural resources in this country.

manage preserve lands. The federal government employs about 75 percent of all people working in land and water conservation.

Land trust and preserve managers must be dedicated to the field of land conservation. They also need the ability to speak and write clearly. They have to be able to juggle many tasks at once and have good people skills in order to work with people from different backgrounds. Land trust and preserve managers who manage the business aspects of their organization should have skills in business administration, finance, and law.

Education and Training

If you are interested in scientific work take biology, chemistry, physics, botany, and ecology classes. All potential land trust or preserve managers can benefit from courses in business, computer science, English, and speech.

A background in biology, chemistry, and physics is important for land trust or preserve managers. A bachelor's degree in a natural science, such as zoology, biology, or botany, is recommended. A master's or a doctorate in a specialty also is a good idea, especially for government positions.

Land trusts need people who are good in business to run the trusts, raise funds, negotiate deals, and handle tax matters. Large land trust organizations also need lawyers, public relations specialists, and others.

Earnings

According to the National Association of Colleges and Employers, graduates with a bachelor's degree in environmental science received average starting salaries of $38,336 in 2007. Earnings for conservation workers range from less than $32,000 to $82,000 or more annually. Conservation professionals with master's degrees and experience earn higher salaries.

Words to Learn

biome a large community of organisms in a single area; examples of biomes are the tropical rain forest, the prairie, the tundra, and the desert

community a group of organisms that share a particular habitat

controlled burn a planned low-intensity fire that is set by professionals to reduce the chance of a larger fire destroying the forest; also called **prescribed burn**

desert a sandy, rocky area that has little vegetation and receives less than 10 inches of rain a year

ecosystem a group of organisms living together with nonliving components

endangered species a species having so few individual survivors that it may become extinct over all or most of its natural range

forest an area with a large number of trees

grazing the process of eating, typically by livestock on rangeland or in farm pastures

habitat an area where an organism or group of organisms normally lives

inventory of species counting the number of different types of plants or animals in a given area

prairie an area with a large number of grasses and related plants; some prairies also may have a few trees

rangeland land that is not farmed or developed; a variety of ecosystems can be found on rangeland

savanna a flat, grassy plain found in tropical areas

tundra a cold region where the soil under the surface of the ground is permanently frozen

watershed the gathering ground of a river system, a ridge that separates two river basins, or an area of land that slopes into a river or lake

wetland an area of land where the soil is saturated with water for all or part of the year

Outlook

Land trusts are growing in popularity. They are the fastest growing segment of the conservation movement today, with

FOR MORE INFO

The following is a national organization of more than 1,665 land trusts nationwide:

Land Trust Alliance
1660 L Street, NW, Suite 1100
Washington, DC 20036-5635
202-638-4725
info@lta.org
http://www.lta.org

The following organization specializes in land trusts and land trust management for areas with rare or endangered species. For information about internships with TNC state chapters or at TNC headquarters, contact

The Nature Conservancy (TNC)
4245 North Fairfax Drive, Suite 100
Arlington, VA 22203-1606
703-841-5300
comment@tnc.org
http://www.nature.org

Contact this organization for information on volunteer positions in natural resource management for high school students.

Student Conservation Association
689 River Road
PO Box 550
Charlestown, NH 03603-0550
603-543-1700
ask-us@thesca.org
http://www.thesca.org

For information about land conservation careers, contact

The Trust for Public Land
116 New Montgomery Street,
Fourth Floor
San Francisco, CA 94105-3638
800-714-LAND
info@tpl.org
http://www.tpl.org

approximately 1,667 in 2005, according to the Land Trust Alliance (LTA). The LTA's National Land Trust Census reports that local, state, and national land trusts protected 37 million acres as of 2005—an increase of 54 percent from 2000.

Currently, private land trusts and national land trust organizations offer the most jobs. Employment growth is expected to be slow with federal land trusts. Those who have both environmental and business training will have the best job prospects.

Marine Biologists

What Marine Biologists Do

Marine biologists are a special type of oceanographer. They study the plants and animals that live in oceans. Marine biologists learn about the tens of thousands of different species that live in salt water.

Marine biologists take sea voyages to study plants and animals in their natural environment. When they reach their destination, perhaps near a coral reef or other habitat, the scientists dive into the water to collect samples.

Because of the cold temperatures below the surface of the sea, marine biologists must wear wetsuits to keep warm. They use scuba gear to help them breathe under water. They may carry a tool, called a slurp gun, which can suck a fish into a specimen bag without hurting it. While underwater, biologists must watch out for dangerous fish and mammals such as sharks or stingrays. They take great care not to hurt the marine environment.

Marine biologists also gather specimens from tidal pools along the shore. They may collect samples at the same time of day for days at a time. They keep samples from different pools separate and carefully write down the pool's location, the types of specimens taken, and their measurements. It is important to keep accurate records.

After they collect specimens, scientists keep them in a special portable aquarium tank on the ship. After returning to land, sometimes weeks or months later, marine biologists study

EXPLORING

- Visit Web sites that focus on oceanography. Interesting sites include Careers in Oceanography, Marine Science, and Marine Biology (http://ocean.peterbrueggeman.com/career.html), MarineBio (http://marinebio.org), and Sea Grant Marine Careers (http://www.marinecareers.net).

- Read books about oceans, marine biology, animals, and careers in the field. Here are a few suggestions: *National Geographic Encyclopedia of Animals,* by Karen McGhee and George McKay (National Geographic Children's Books, 2006); *Oceans,* by Beverly McMillan and John A. Musick (Simon & Schuster Children's Publishing, 2007); *Opportunities in Marine Science and Maritime Careers,* by William Ray Heitzmann (McGraw-Hill, 2006); and *You Can Be a Woman Marine Biologist,* by Florence McAlary and Judith Love Cohen (Cascade Pass Inc., 2001).

- Visit your local aquarium to learn about marine life and about the life of a marine biologist.

- If you live near the ocean, you can collect shells and other specimens. Keep a notebook to record details about what you find and where.

- You can begin diving training while in high school. Between the ages of 10 and 14 you can earn a Junior Open Water Diver certification from PADI. This allows you to dive in the company of a certified adult. When you turn 15, you can upgrade your certification to Open Water Diver.

- Talk to a marine biologist about his or her career. Ask the following questions: What made you want to become a marine biologist? What do you like most and least about your job? What is your favorite marine animal to study? How did you train to become a marine biologist? What advice would you give to someone who is interested in the career?

the specimens in their laboratories. They might check the amount of oxygen in a sea turtle's blood stream to learn how the turtles can stay underwater for so long. Or they might measure the blood chemistry of an arctic fish to discover how it can survive very cold temperatures.

Marine biologists study changing conditions of the ocean, such as temperature or chemicals that have polluted the water. They try to see how those changes affect the plants and animals that live there. If certain species become extinct or are no longer safe to eat (because of pollution), the world's food supply grows smaller.

Tips for Success

To be a successful marine biologist, you should

- enjoy asking questions to solve problems
- be able to observe small details carefully
- enjoy conducting research
- like math and science
- be a good diver
- enjoy being outdoors in all types of weather
- have good communication skills

The work of these scientists is also important for improving and managing sport and commercial fishing. Through underwater exploration, marine biologists have discovered that humans are destroying the world's coral reefs. They have also charted the migration of whales and counted the decreasing numbers of certain species. They have seen dolphins being caught by accident in tuna fishermen's nets. By telling people about their discoveries through written reports and research papers, marine biologists sometimes help people and governments make changes that protect the environment.

In addition to conducting research in the field, marine biologists also teach marine biology at colleges and universities. Some marine biologists write books and articles about the field and appear as scientific experts in documentaries.

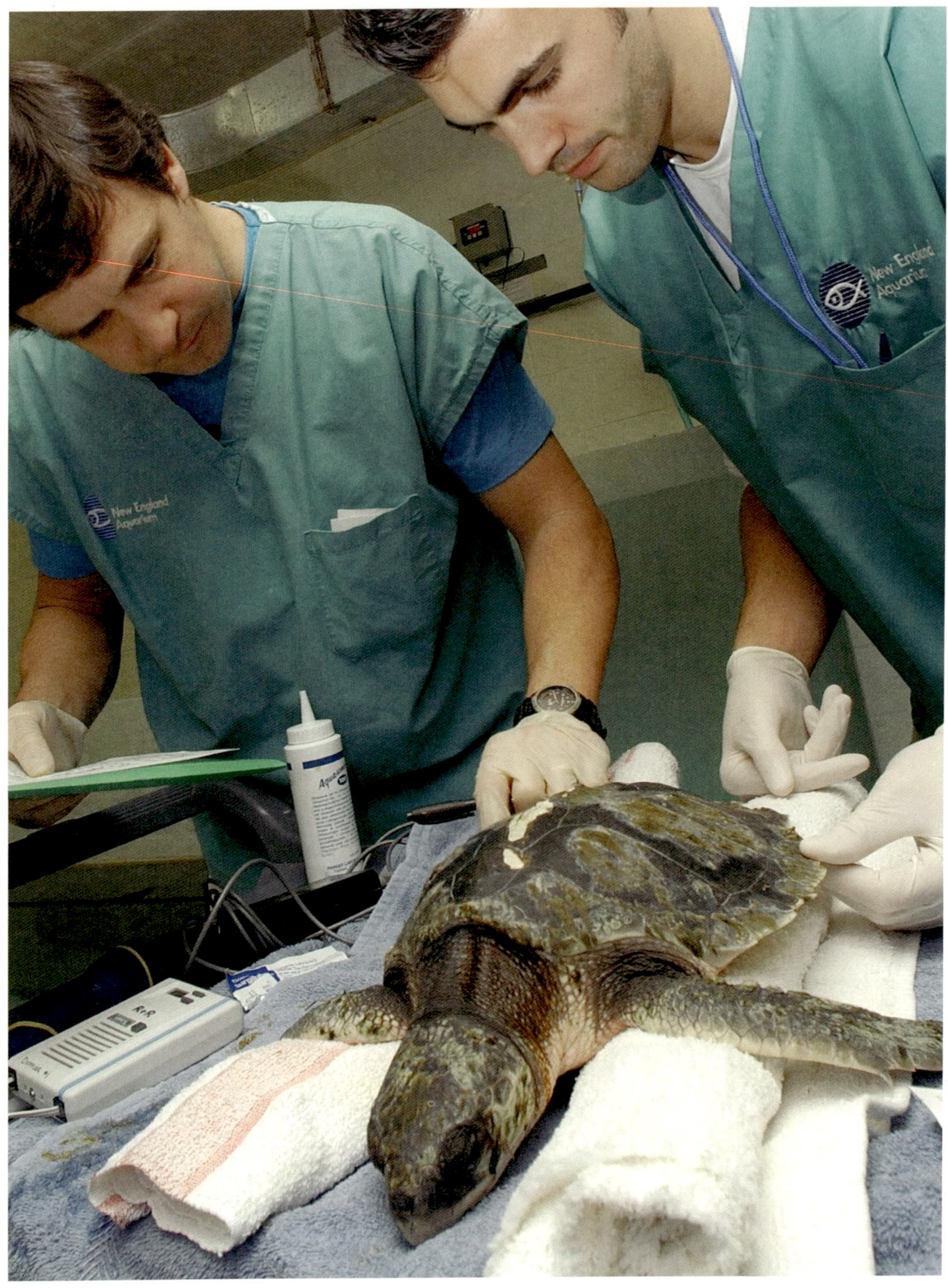

A marine biologist (left) *and a volunteer at the New England Aquarium examine a Kemp's ridley sea turtle.* (Michael Dwyer, AP Photo)

Education and Training

If you want to be a marine biologist, you should like math and science. Biology, botany, and chemistry classes are important to take in high school. Although you can get a job as a marine biologist with a bachelor's degree, most marine biologists have a master's or doctoral degree.

Earnings

Salaries vary depending on how much education and experience you have. The average wildlife biologist earned about $55,000 in 2008, according to the U.S. Department of Labor. Those just starting out in the field earned less than $33,000. Those with

Words to Learn

community a group of organisms that share a particular habitat

coral reef a living structure in the ocean that is made out of the exoskeletons of a tiny organism called a coral polyp

ecosystem a group of organisms living together with nonliving components

habitat an area where an organism or group of organisms normally lives

inventory of species counting the number of different types of plants or animals in a given area

migration the mass movement of a group of organisms during which normal behaviors such as breeding are ignored; migration often occurs as a result of the changing of the seasons

specimen a small sample of a living organism or nonliving object

tidal pool a pool of seawater left on rocks near the ocean shore when the water (or tide) recedes; a variety of animals live in these temporary pools, including crabs, starfish, barnacles, small fish, and sea urchins

wetsuit a garment that protects the wearer from the harsh conditions of the ocean or other bodies of water

FOR MORE INFO

For information on careers and marine science, contact the following organizations:

American Institute of Biological Sciences
1444 I Street, NW, Suite 200
Washington, DC 20005-6535
202-628-1500
http://www.aibs.org

American Society of Limnology and Oceanography
5400 Bosque Boulevard, Suite 680
Waco, TX 76710-4446
800-929-2756
http://www.aslo.org

For ocean news, contact
The Oceanography Society
PO Box 1931
Rockville, MD 20849-1931
301-251-7708
info@tos.org
http://www.tos.org

For information on diving instruction and certification, contact
PADI
30151 Tomas Street
Rancho Santa Margarita, CA 92688-2125
800-729-7234
http://www.padi.com

doctorates in marine biology or a lot of experience earned more than $91,000 a year. Senior scientists or full professors at universities can earn more than $110,000 a year.

Outlook

Many people want to work as marine biologists—especially in top positions. Opportunities in research are especially hard to find. Those who have advanced degrees and specialized knowledge in math and computer science will have the best chances for employment. Changes in the earth's environment, such as global warming, lead to a need for more research and so create more jobs. Marine biologists should be able to find jobs managing the world's fisheries, making medicines from marine organisms, and growing marine food alternatives, such as seaweed and plankton.

Naturalists

What Naturalists Do

Naturalists study the natural world. They do so in order to learn the best way to preserve the earth and living creatures of all varieties. They teach the public about the environment and show people what they can do about such hazards as pollution.

Naturalists also can work as *nature resource managers, wildlife conservationists, ecologists,* and *environmental educators* for many different employers.

Depending on where they work, naturalists may protect and conserve wildlife or particular kinds of land, such as prairie or wetlands. Other naturalists research and carry out plans to restore lands that have been damaged by erosion, fire, or development. Some naturalists recreate wildlife habitats and nature trails. They plant trees, for example, or label existing plants (so hikers and campers know what they are). *Fish and wildlife wardens* help manage populations of fish, hunted animals, and protected animals. They control hunting and fishing and make sure species are thriving but not overpopulating their territories. Overpopulation happens when too many of one type of plant or animal takes over an area. *Wildlife managers, range managers,* and *conservationists* also maintain the plant and animal life in a certain area. They work in parks or on ranges that have both domestic livestock

75

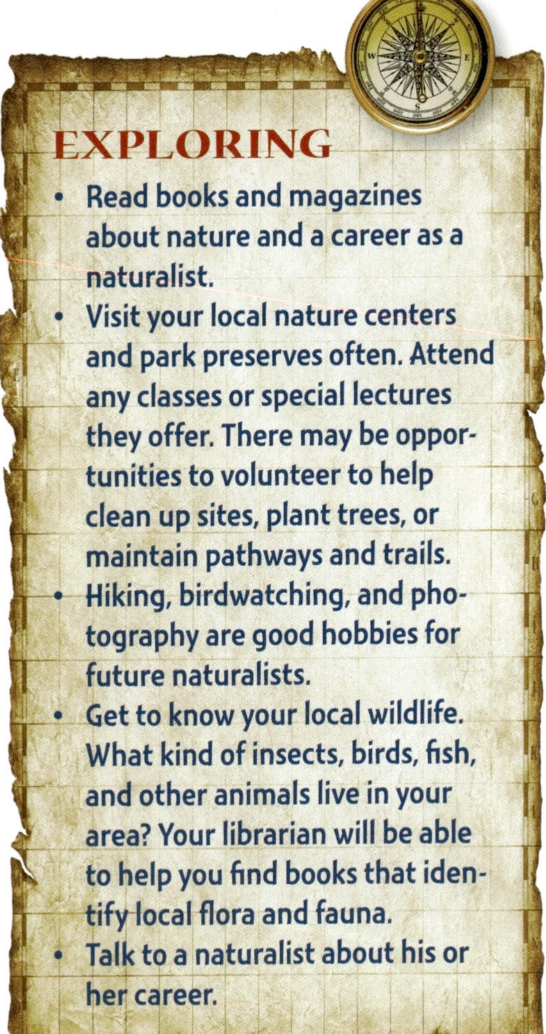

EXPLORING

- Read books and magazines about nature and a career as a naturalist.
- Visit your local nature centers and park preserves often. Attend any classes or special lectures they offer. There may be opportunities to volunteer to help clean up sites, plant trees, or maintain pathways and trails.
- Hiking, birdwatching, and photography are good hobbies for future naturalists.
- Get to know your local wildlife. What kind of insects, birds, fish, and other animals live in your area? Your librarian will be able to help you find books that identify local flora and fauna.
- Talk to a naturalist about his or her career.

(animals such as cattle that have been tamed by humans) and wild animals (such as deer, bears, and coyotes). They test soil and water for pollution and nutrients. They count plant and animal populations each season.

Naturalists also work indoors. They raise money for projects, write reports, keep detailed records, and write articles, brochures, and newsletters to tell the public about their work. They might try to rally for support for protection of an endangered species by holding meetings and hearings. Other public education activities include leading tours and nature walks and holding demonstrations, exhibits, and classes.

Naturalists are employed in wildlife museums, private nature centers, large zoos, parks and nature preserves, arboretums, botanical gardens, and government agencies such as the U.S. Fish and Wildlife Service or the National Park Service.

Naturalists should enjoy working outdoors since they spend the majority of their time outside in all kinds of weather. They should also be able to work well with other environmental professionals and the general public. They should be good teachers in order to educate the public about nature and environmental issues. Finally, naturalists should have good writing skills. They need these to prepare educational materials and grant proposals.

Education and Training

If you are interested in this field, you should take basic science courses in high school, including biology, chemistry, and earth science. Botany courses and clubs are also helpful, since they will give you direct experience observing plant growth and health.

Naturalists must have at least a bachelor's degree in biology, zoology, chemistry, botany, natural history, or environmental science. A master's degree is not required, but is helpful. Many naturalists have a master's degree in education. Experience gained through summer jobs and volunteer work can be just as important as educational requirements. Experience working with the public is also helpful.

Earnings

Starting salaries for full-time naturalists range from about $20,000 to $29,000 per year. Some part-time workers, however, earn as little as minimum wage ($7.25 per hour). For some positions, housing and vehicles may be provided. Earnings vary for those with more duties or advanced degrees. The U.S. Department of Labor reports that conservation scientists (a career

Profile: Terry Tempest Williams (1955–)

Terry Tempest Williams is an American naturalist, writer, and environmental activist. She is best known for her works about natural places in the American West. Her writings and advocacy are credited with inspiring President Clinton to establish the Grand Staircase-Escalante National Monument in Utah. Some of Williams' books include *Refuge: An Unnatural History of Family and Place; An Unspoken Hunger: Stories from the Field; Desert Quartet; Red: Passion and Patience in the Desert; The Open Space of Democracy;* and *Mosaic: Finding Beauty in a Broken World.* In 2006, Williams received the Robert Marshall Award from The Wilderness Society. It is the highest honor given to an American citizen. Visit http://www.coyoteclan.com to learn more about her career.

The Young Naturalist Awards

If you are in grades seven through 12, you can participate in the Young Naturalist Awards—a competition that is held by the American Museum of Natural History. To compete, you need to "plan and conduct your own scientific investigation, one that will include questions, hypotheses, and trips into the field to gather data." No one is expecting you to make a new scientific discovery. Instead, your investigation should help you better understand a part of the natural world. Sample questions might include: How many trees are in my neighborhood?

Is our local creek polluted? What do leopard frogs like to eat? When do deer sleep? You compete for the award by writing an essay about your research and the results of your investigation. You can also include photos that show your work. This contest is a great way to develop your scientific skills and explore the world around you. Winners receive a cash prize. Visit http://www.amnh. org/nationalcenter/youngnatural- istawards to learn more about this exciting contest and to read past winning essays.

category that includes naturalists) earned an average annual salary of $58,720 in 2008. Conservation scientists employed by the federal government earned mean annual salaries of $69,090, and those employed by social advocacy organizations earned $54,540. Conservation scientists employed at colleges and universities earned $54,620. Experienced conservation scientists made $87,000 or more.

Outlook

In the next decade, the job outlook for naturalists is expected to be only fair, despite the public's increasing interest in the environment. Private nature centers and preserves—where forests,

FOR MORE INFO

For information on careers, contact
American Society of Naturalists
http://www.amnat.org

For information about career opportunities, contact
Bureau of Land Management
U.S. Department of the Interior
1849 C Street, Room 5665
Washington, DC 20240-0001
202-208-3801
http://www.blm.gov

For information about conservation programs, contact
National Wildlife Federation
11100 Wildlife Center Drive
Reston, VA 20190-5362
800-822-9919
http://www.nwf.org

For information about conservation and volunteer opportunities, contact
Student Conservation Association
689 River Road
PO Box 550
Charlestown, NH 03603-0550
603-543-1700
ask-us@thesca.org
http://www.thesca.org

For information about careers, contact
U.S. Fish and Wildlife Service
U.S. Department of the Interior
4401 North Fairfax Drive
Arlington, VA 22203-1610
http://www.fws.gov/jobs

wetlands, and prairies are restored—are continuing to open in the United States. But possible government cutbacks in the amount of money provided to nature programs may limit their growth. Many people want to enter this field, which will make it difficult to land a job.

Oceanographers

What Oceanographers Do

Oceanographers are scientists who study the oceans. They conduct experiments and gather information about the water, plant and animal life, and the ocean floor. They study the motion of waves, currents (a strong flow of water in a body of water), and tides (the regular rise and fall of water in an ocean or lake). They also look at water temperature, the chemical makeup of the ocean water, and pollution levels at different depths of the oceans.

Oceanographers use several inventions specially designed for long- and short-term underwater observation. They use deep-sea equipment, such as submarines and observation tanks. Underwater devices called bathyspheres allow an oceanographer to stay underwater for several hours or even days. For short observations or to explore areas such as underwater caves, scientists use deep-sea and scuba diving gear that straps onto the body to supply them with oxygen.

Oceanographers do most of their work out on the water. While at sea, they gather the scientific information that they need. Then they spend months or years in offices, laboratories, or libraries studying the data. Oceanographers use information such as water temperature changes between the surface and the lower depths to predict droughts and monsoon rains. Droughts are periods of time when there is little or no rain. Monsoon rains are heavy rains that can cause major flooding and damage.

Most oceanographers specialize in one of four areas.

EXPLORING

- Visit Web sites that focus on oceanography. Interesting sites include Careers in Oceanography, Marine Science, and Marine Biology (http://ocean.peterbrueggeman.com/career.html), MarineBio.org (http://marinebio.org), and Sea Grant Marine Careers (http://www.marinecareers.net).
- If you live near coastal regions, it will be easier to learn about oceans and ocean life. Read all you can about rocks, minerals, and aquatic life. If you live or travel near an oceanography research center, such as Woods Hole Oceanographic Institution (http://www.whoi.edu) on Cape Cod in Massachusetts, spend some time studying its exhibits.
- If you do not live near water, try to find summer camps or programs that make trips to coastal areas. Learn all you can about the geology, atmosphere, and plant and animal life of the area where you live, regardless of whether water is present.
- Ask a counselor or teacher to help arrange an information interview with an oceanographer.

Those who study ocean plants and animals are called *biological oceanographers* or *marine biologists.* They collect information on the behavior and activities of the wildlife in a specific area of the ocean.

Physical oceanographers study ocean temperature and the atmosphere above the water. They study the greenhouse effect, or the warming of the planet's surface. They calculate the movement of the warm water (known as a current) through the oceans to help meteorologists predict weather patterns.

Geological oceanographers study the ocean floor. They use instruments that monitor the ocean floor and the minerals

An oceanographer (left) *travels to an island to conduct research.* (Al Grillo, AP Photo)

found there from a far distance. In areas where the ocean is too deep for any human-made equipment to go, they use remote sensors.

Geochemical oceanographers study the chemical makeup of ocean water and the ocean floor. They study pollution problems and possible chemical causes for plant and animal diseases in a particular region of the water. Geochemical oceanographers are called in after oil spills to check the level of damage to the water and ecosystem.

About 18 percent of oceanographers work for federal or state governments. Federal employers of oceanographers include the Environmental Protection Agency, the Department of Defense, the National Park Service, and the Biological Resources Discipline of the U.S. Geological Survey, among others. State governments often employ oceanographers in environmental agencies or state-funded research projects. About 40 percent of oceanographers work for colleges or universities as teachers and researchers. Other oceanographers work for private industries such as non-profit organizations, oil and gas extraction companies, and industrial firms.

Tips for Success

To be a successful oceanographer, you should

- **have a strong interest in science, especially the physical and earth sciences**
- **have a curious nature**
- **enjoy being outdoors**
- **enjoy observing nature and performing experiments**
- **like reading, researching, and writing**
- **have good communication skills**
- **be able to work well with others**

Education and Training

Science courses, including geology, biology, and chemistry, and math classes, such as algebra, trigonometry, and statistics, are especially important to take in high school. Because your work will involve a great deal of research and documentation, take English classes to improve your research and communication skills. In addition, take computer science classes because you will use computers throughout your professional life.

To become an oceanographer, you will need at least a bachelor's degree in chemistry, biology, geology, or physics. For most research or teaching positions, you will need a master's degree or doctoral degree in oceanography.

Earnings

According to the National Association of Colleges and Employers, students graduating with a bachelor's degree in geology

DID YOU KNOW?

The blue whale is the largest animal on earth. Some say it is the biggest animal that has ever lived—larger than the biggest dinosaurs! The longest blue whale ever recorded was 108 feet in length. Blue whales can weigh 100 to 150 tons. They mainly eat krill, which are small, shrimp-like organisms. During the summer feeding season, blue whales can eat up to 40 million krill a day. Blue whales live in every type of ocean around the world—from polar waters in the Arctic to the tropical waters of the Caribbean.

By the early 1930s, blue whales were nearly hunted to extinction. In 1966, the International Whaling Commission banned the hunting of these whales throughout the world. Since then, blue whale populations have recovered very slowly. It is estimated that there are only 8,000 to 14,000 blue whales left in the entire world. Before they were hunted, experts estimate that there were 350,000 blue whales.

Visit the American Cetacean Society's Web site, http://www.acsonline.org/factpack/bluewhl.htm, to learn about these beautiful, and endangered, marine mammals.

and related sciences were offered an average starting salary of $40,786 in 2007. Salaries for geoscientists (a category that includes the career of oceanographer) ranged from less than $42,000 to more than $155,000 in 2008, with a median of $79,160, according to the U.S. Department of Labor. The average salary for experienced oceanographers working for the federal government was about $91,000.

Outlook

Employment for all geoscientists (including oceanographers) is expected to be good in the coming years. Although the field of marine science is growing, researchers specializing in the popular field of biological oceanography, or marine biology, will face competition for available positions and research funding. However, because more people want to understand and protect

FOR MORE INFO

For information about careers, education, and publications, contact
American Society of Limnology and Oceanography
5400 Bosque Boulevard, Suite 680
Waco, TX 76710-4446
800-929-2756
http://www.aslo.org

For information on how to join the MTS Club (for students in grades six-12), contact
Marine Technology Society (MTS)
5565 Sterrett Place, Suite 108
Columbia, MD 21044-2606

410-884-5330
http://www.mtsociety.org

For ocean news, contact
The Oceanography Society
PO Box 1931
Rockville, MD 20849-1931
301-251-7708
info@tos.org
http://www.tos.org

the environment there will be more jobs available. There will be more opportunities for oceanographers who study global climate change and fisheries science, as well as conduct marine biomedical and pharmaceutical research. Oceanographers who can speak a foreign language and who don't mind working outside the United States will have good job prospects.

What Park Rangers Do

Park rangers protect animals and preserve forests, ponds, rivers, and other natural resources. They teach visitors about parks by giving lectures and tours. They also make sure rules and regulations are followed to maintain a safe environment for visitors and wildlife. For example, they make sure that visitors stay on trails away from dangerous geysers or hot springs and do not get too close to bears or herds of buffalo. They also police the park to ensure that people are not driving motorized vehicles in areas where their presence could damage plants or wildlife or otherwise breaking park regulations. The National Park Service is one of the major employers of park rangers. In addition, park rangers work for other federal land and resource management agencies and similar state and local agencies.

Safety is a key responsibility for park rangers. They often require visitors to register at park offices so they will know when the visitors are expected to return from a hike or other activity. Rangers know first aid and, if there is an accident or animal attack, they may have to help visitors who have been hurt. Rangers carefully mark hiking trails and other areas to reduce the risk of injuries for visitors and to protect plants and animals.

Rangers help visitors enjoy and learn about parks. They give lectures and provide guided tours of the park, explaining why certain plants and animals live there. They might explain how and why wolves were reintroduced into Yellowstone National Park. Others may talk about efforts to protect the Shenandoah

EXPLORING

- Read as much as you can about local, state, and national parks. The National Park Service's Web site, http://www.nps.gov, is a great place to start.
- If you are between the ages of five and 12, you can become a junior ranger at a National Park near you. Visit http://www.nps.gov/learn for details. If there isn't a participating park in your area, you can still get involved by becoming a Web ranger. Visit http://www.nps.gov/webrangers for more information.
- Get to know your local wildlife. What kind of insects, mammals, birds, fish, and other animals live in your area? Your science teacher or librarian will be able to help you find books that identify local flora and fauna.
- Hands-on experience can be a great advantage if you are interested in entering this competitive field. You can get this experience by getting involved in the Volunteers-in-Parks (VIP) program, which is sponsored by the National Park Service. Park volunteers help park employees in any number of ways, including answering phone calls, welcoming visitors, maintaining trails, building fences, painting buildings, or picking up litter. There are also other volunteer opportunities for people ages five through 24. For more information, visit http://www.nps.gov/volunteer.
- You also may be able to volunteer at state, county, or local parks. Universities and conservation organizations often have volunteer groups that work on research activities, studies, and rehabilitation efforts.
- Talk to a park ranger about his or her career.

salamander, which only lives on three mountains in Shenandoah National Park or the Pecos sunflower, a threatened plant that is found in El Malpais National Monument.

A ranger shows photographs of bears to tourists in Yellowstone National Park. (Douglas C. Pizac, AP Photo)

Research and conservation efforts are also a big part of a park ranger's responsibilities. They study wildlife behavior by tagging and following certain animals. (Tagging involves placing an electronic collar or tracking device on an animal.) They may investigate sources of pollution that come from outside the park. Then they develop plans to help reduce pollution to make the park a better place for plants, animals, and visitors.

Rangers also do bookkeeping and other paperwork. They issue permits to visitors and keep track of how many people use the park. They also plan recreational activities and decide how to spend the money budgeted to the park.

Education and Training

In high school, take courses in earth science, biology, mathematics, history, English, and speech. Any classes or activities that deal with plant and animal life, the weather, geography, history, and interacting with others will be helpful.

Park rangers usually have bachelor's degrees in natural resource, wildlife management, or recreational resource management. A degree in many other fields, such as biology or ecology, is also acceptable. Without a degree, you need at least three years of experience working in parks or conservation.

Earnings

In 2009, new rangers in the National Park Service earned between $27,026 and $35,135 annually. Rangers with some experience earned between $33,477 and $43,521. The most experienced rangers who supervise other workers earn more than $90,000 a year. The government may provide housing to rangers who work in remote areas. Rangers in state parks earn average starting salaries of about $25,000.

DID YOU KNOW?

Today, national parks in the United States cover more than 84 million acres of mountains, plains, deserts, swamps, historic sites, lakeshores, forests, rivers, battlefields, memorials, archaeological properties, and recreation areas.

Tips for Success

To be a successful park ranger, you should

- be interested in protecting plants and animals
- be a good teacher
- enjoy working outdoors
- have a pleasant personality
- be able to work with many different kinds of people
- be in good physical shape
- be able to enforce park rules and regulations
- be willing to travel to take on new assignments

FOR MORE INFO

For information about state parks and employment opportunities, contact
National Association of State Park Directors
8829 Woodyhill Road
Raleigh, NC 27613-1134
919-676-8365
NASPD@me.com
http://www.naspd.org

For general career information, contact the following organizations:
National Parks Conservation Association
1300 19th Street, NW, Suite 300
Washington, DC 20036-1628
800-628-7275
npca@npca.org
http://www.npca.org

National Recreation and Park Association
22377 Belmont Ridge Road
Ashburn, VA 20148-4501
800-626-6772
info@nrpa.org
http://www.nrpa.org

For information about careers with the National Park Service, contact
National Park Service
U.S. Department of the Interior
1849 C Street, NW
Washington, DC 20240-0001
202-208-6843
http://www.nps.gov

Contact this organization for information on volunteer positions in natural resource management for high school students.
Student Conservation Association
689 River Road
PO Box 550
Charlestown, NH 03603-0550
603-543-1700
ask-us@thesca.org
http://www.thesca.org

Outlook

Many people want to become park rangers. In fact, there are not enough jobs for everyone who wants to enter the field. Park ranger jobs should continue to be popular in the future. Because of this stiff competition for positions, the job outlook is expected to change little. As a result, those interested in the field should attain the greatest number and widest variety of skills possible. They may wish to study subjects they can use in other fields, such as forestry, land management, conservation, wildlife management, history, and natural sciences.

Recycling Coordinators

What Recycling Coordinators Do

You have probably been asked by your parents or teachers to recycle cans, plastic containers, newspapers, and other items. By doing so, you are protecting the environment and conserving valuable resources. For example, every time you recycle a bottle, there is one less bottle in a landfill and one less bottle that has to be manufactured from scratch. This makes our planet a cleaner place.

Recycling coordinators manage the recycling programs of counties, cities, and towns. They make sure city workers or private contractors collect, sort, and process recyclable materials. They also may help find new markets for recyclables, manage a staff, and report to local authorities. Some coordinators promote recycling programs in their communities.

In the mid-1960s garbage was piling up in a lot of major cities, and authorities were not doing a good job of managing the trash. In an effort to solve this problem, federal and state laws established new requirements for handling municipal solid waste (MSW). Today, most U.S. municipalities want to keep as much MSW out of landfills and incinerators as possible. Landfills are places where waste is buried. They can leak hazardous substances into surrounding land and release toxic emissions. Incinerators are used to burn trash, and they, too, can release toxic emissions. When more trash is recycled, less has to be burned or buried.

Each recycling program differs according to the community, location, population, funding, and other factors. Source

EXPLORING

- Read industry-related magazines. Two informative publications are *Recycling Today* (http://www.recyclingtoday.com) and *Resource Recycling* (http://www.resource-recycling.com).
- Start recycling at home. Visit the following Web sites to help you get started: http://www.nrc-recycle.org/consumers.aspx, http://www.container-recycling.org/kids.htm, http://www.epa.gov/kids/garbage.htm, http://kids.niehs.nih.gov/recycle.htm, and http://www.paperrecycles.org.
- You can start to explore a career as a recycling coordinator by getting familiar with the issues. Why is sorting garbage so costly? Why are some materials recycled and not others? Where are the markets? What are some creative uses for recyclable materials? Find out what's going on both nationally and in your area.
- Volunteer to help with fund drives and information campaigns for a recycling organization.
- Ask your teacher or counselor to arrange a tour of a local material recovery facility, where you can see recycling firsthand and talk with the staff there.

reduction is part of many of these plans. This means discouraging people from throwing out a lot of trash in the first place. Some cities pick up just one bag of trash per household per week and charge a fee for more bags. Other communities limit or ban disposal of certain wastes. To collect recyclables, some communities have drop-off points where residents can bring paper, glass, aluminum, or other materials. Others ask people to put recyclables in special bags or containers and throw them out with the rest of the trash. Paper, glass, plastic, and aluminum are the materials most often recycled. Other materials that can be recycled include animal waste, yard waste, appliances, wood wastes (such as shipping pallets and boxes), motor oil, scrap metal, and tires. In the future, experts believe that far more materials will be recycled.

Recycling coordinators are in charge of educating the public about the recycling programs that are available in their communities. They encourage people to recycle by keeping them informed of what materials can be recycled, how they should be packaged, and where and when to deposit them.

> **DID YOU KNOW?**
>
> According to the National Recycling Coalition, the recycling and reuse industry consists of approximately 56,000 companies that employ more than 1.1 million people, generate an annual payroll of nearly $37 billion, and gross more than $236 billion in annual revenues.

Education and Training

To prepare for this career, focus your high school studies on business, economics, English, math, and science. Learning about the environment will you give a general overview of why recycling is so important.

A bachelor's degree in environmental studies or a related area, plus business experience and proven communication skills, is desirable. Some colleges and universities are developing a minor in integrated waste management.

Earnings

Salaries vary widely for recycling coordinators. Starting salaries range from $22,000 per

> **Tips for Success**
>
> To be a successful recycling coordinator, you should
>
> - have good communication skills
> - be able to work well with people from different backgrounds
> - have excellent leadership and management abilities
> - be able to convince others to recycle
> - have good organization skills

FOR MORE INFO

For information about container recycling, contact
Container Recycling Institute
4361 Keystone Avenue
Culver City, CA 90232-3436
310-559-7451
http://www.container-recycling.org

This organization provides technical information, education, training, outreach and advocacy services. Visit its Web site for information on recycling.
National Recycling Coalition
805 15th Street, NW, Suite 425
Washington, DC 20005-2239
202-789-1430
info@nrc-recycle.org
http://www.nrc-recycle.org

year in smaller counties or cities to $75,000 and higher for coordinators in larger municipalities. Experienced recycling coordinators earn more than $100,000.

Outlook

Opportunities for recycling coordinators should be good during the next decade. The waste management and recycling industries will need more people to run recovery facilities, design new recycling technologies, come up with new ways to use recyclables, and do related work. Private businesses are also expected to hire recycling coordinators to manage in-house programs.

Opportunities for recycling coordinators may be reduced if government agencies do not have enough funding to operate recycling programs.

Renewable Energy Workers

What Renewable Energy Workers Do

Much of our energy in the United States comes from oil, coal, and natural gas. But in recent years, many people have begun to realize that mining and using these resources is causing very serious damage to our environment. Plus, we will not be able to use oil, coal, and natural gas forever to fuel our cars, heat our houses, and provide electricity. These nonrenewable resources will run out someday, and we will have to rely on renewable energy resources. Renewable energy is power or fuel that comes from wind, sunlight (solar), water (hydro), organic matter (biomass), and the earth's internal heat (geothermal).

Wind energy is generated by wind turbines. Wind plants, or wind farms, have many of these turbines, which can generate electricity for tens of thousands of homes. *Electrical, mechanical,* and *aeronautical engineers* design and test the turbines as well as the wind farms. *Meteorologists* help identify prime locations for new project sites and serve as consultants on projects. Skilled *construction workers* build the farms. *Windsmiths,* sometimes called *mechanical* or *electrical technicians,* operate and maintain the turbines and other equipment on the farm.

The most common solar energy technology today uses photovoltaic (PV) cells, which absorb sunlight and turn it into electricity. Electrical, mechanical, and *chemical engineers* work in research and development departments. *Architects,* many of whom specialize in passive solar design and construction, design solar-powered structures. Technicians, *electricians, installers,* and construction workers build and maintain solar projects.

EXPLORING

- Read as much as you can about renewable energy in books and magazines and on the Web. Here is one book suggestion: *Careers in Renewable Energy: Get a Green Energy Job*, by Gregory McNamee (Pixy-Jack Press, 2008).
- Volunteering is one way to explore the renewable energy industry. You can find energy fairs or conventions in your area by contacting energy associations. Your duties may consist of handing out brochures or acting as a gofer, but you'll make many industry contacts.
- Some professional associations have student chapters or junior clubs. In addition to providing information about different careers in renewable energy, student chapters promote contests and offer information on scholarships and internships.
- Industry associations also hold many competitions designed to promote their particular renewable energy sector. One such contest is the Junior Solar Sprint (http://www.nesea.org/k-12/juniorsolarsprint) for junior high school students. The contest, which is sponsored by the Northeast Sustainable Energy Association and the U.S. Army, calls for the construction and racing of solar-powered model cars. Contestants learn about renewable energy technologies and concepts in a fun, challenging, and exciting setting.
- Talk to a renewable energy worker about his or her career.

Hydropower uses the energy of flowing water to produce electricity. Electrical and mechanical engineers and technicians design, construct, and maintain hydropower projects. *Biologists* and other *environmental scientists* assess the effects of hydropower projects on wildlife and the environment. *Recreation man-*

agers and *trail planners* manage and preserve the land surrounding reservoirs or dams.

Bioenergy is the energy stored in biomass—organic matter such as trees, straw, or corn. Bioenergy can be used directly, as in burning wood for cooking or heating purposes, or indirectly, as in the production of electricity using wood waste as a source of power. *Chemists, biochemists, biologists,* and *agricultural scientists* work together to find faster and less costly ways to produce bioenergy. Engineers, construction workers, electricians, and technicians build and maintain bioenergy conversion plants. *Farmers* and *foresters* raise and harvest crops or other sources of biomass.

Geothermal heat comes from the heat within the earth. Water heated from geothermal energy is tapped from its underground reservoirs and used to heat buildings, grow crops, or melt snow. Geothermal energy can also be used to generate electricity. The geothermal industry employs *geologists, geochemists,* and *geophysicists* to research and locate new reservoirs. *Hydraulic engineers, reservoir engineers,* and *drillers* work together to reach and maintain the reservoir's heat supply. The building of new geothermal projects requires the work of electricians, *welders, mechanics,* and *construction workers. Drilling workers, machinists,* and *mechanics* maintain drilling equipment.

Renewable energy professionals are employed by for-profit companies, nonprofit renewable energy organizations, government agencies, and colleges and universities. Some are self-employed and work as consultants.

Tips for Success

To be a successful renewable energy worker, you should

- care about protecting the environment
- be interested in renewable energy
- be able to work as a member of a team
- have good time-management skills
- be organized
- have excellent communication skills
- be willing to continue to learn throughout your career

A technician installs a photovoltaic panel. (National Renewable Energy Laboratory)

Education and Training

For many jobs in the renewable energy industry, it pays to have a strong background in science and mathematics. For example, earth science, agriculture, and biology classes will be useful if you plan to work in the hydropower industry researching the effects of a new hydropower project on the surrounding plant and animal life. Math, earth science, and chemistry classes will be helpful if you plan to work in the geothermal energy industry identifying and harvesting possible sources of geothermal energy from within the earth. Physics classes will be helpful if you plan to work in the wind industry designing windmills and turbine engines to capture and convert wind energy into electricity.

However, you need not be technically gifted in science and math in order to succeed in the renewable energy industry. Computer classes are useful for workers who run design programs, organize research, and maintain basic office records. Finance, accounting, communications, and English classes will be helpful to anyone who is interested in working in the business end of the industry. Taking a foreign language is highly useful since a majority of renewable energy companies are located outside of the United States.

A strong background in science and mathematics is necessary for many jobs in the renewable energy industry. Most technical jobs require at least an associate's or bachelor's degree. Courses of study range from environmental science and mathematics to architecture and meteorology. Research and development workers usually have bachelor's or master's degrees in electrical, chemical, or mechanical engineering. Some scientists have graduate degrees in engineering or the sciences (such as biology, physics, or chemistry). Some colleges are beginning to offer degrees in renewable energy or in specialties such as solar or wind energy.

Earnings

The U.S. Department of Labor does not provide information on salaries in the renewable energy industry. However, it does report that the mean salary for electrical engineers employed in electric power generation, transmission, and distribution (a field that is linked to the renewable energy industry) was $84,450 in

Fame & Fortune: T. Boone Pickens

T. Boone Pickens is a well-known businessman who has made hundreds of millions of dollars in the oil and natural gas industries. Since the use of oil and gas can often hurt the environment, it might be surprising that he would be featured in a book about the environment. But in recent years, Pickens has created a plan to develop wind and solar energy that will help the United States stop being dependent on other countries for our energy. The development of these renewable energy technologies will also create jobs and help protect the environment.

Pickens was born in 1928 in Holdenville, Oklahoma. He always had a knack for business. As a teen, he expanded his newspaper delivery business by buying up other routes whenever possible. Pickens had good business skills and always wanted to develop and manage his own business. As a young man, he left his first adult employer, Phillips Petroleum, and started his own company with only $2,500 and a lot of determination and hard work. He built this company into a very successful business. Pickens had a long career in the oil and natural and gas industries, with many highs and lows.

In 2008, when most men his age would be retired, Pickens spent millions of his own money to introduce the Pickens Plan to the American public. The plan seeks to solve America's energy problems by creating a giant wind farm in Texas to generate renewable energy and promote the use of solar energy. Pickens hopes to convince lawmakers and the general public to build a network of wind farms from Texas north to the Canadian border and beyond (areas that have a high amount of wind).

Pickens was named to the 2009 *Time* 100, a list of the most influential people in the world. The American Wind Energy Association named Pickens its 2009 Industry Person of the Year for "his vision and leadership in moving the wind industry forward." Visit http://www.boonepickens.com for more information.

Sources: *Time,* Boonepickens.com

2008. Salaries for all electrical engineers ranged from less than $52,000 to more than $125,000.

Annual salaries for nontechnical workers vary according to the position, type and size of the employer, and job responsibili-

Top 5 Ways to Reduce Global Warming

1. Buy reusable products instead of disposable ones. Purchase products with less packaging to reduce the amount of waste. Recycle newspaper, paper, plastic, aluminum, and glass. Start a recycling program at your school.
2. Weatherproof your house to save money on heating and cooling costs. Adjust your thermostat (lower in winter and higher in the summer) to reduce the use of fossil fuels and help save money on your utility bills.
3. Use compact fluorescent light bulbs in place of regular light bulbs.
4. Reduce emissions by asking your parents to drive less and walk more. Make sure that your family car is in top shape to improve gas mileage.
5. Ask your parents to purchase energy-efficient cars and appliances.

Source: About.com

ties. The average office worker might earn a salary that ranges from $20,000 to $50,000. A typical administrative position would probably pay salaries ranging from $25,000 to $75,000. Those employed by nonprofit organizations tend to earn slightly less than those who work at corporations.

Outlook

The wind industry is the fastest growing sector of the renewable energy industry. Employment is expected to be very good during the next decade, especially for windsmiths, engineers, meteorologists, electricians, and other technical workers.

The solar energy industry is also experiencing strong growth. The need to manufacture and install photovoltaic cell systems will create many employment opportunities.

FOR MORE INFO

For information about careers, employment opportunities, and industry surveys, contact
Association of Energy Engineers
4025 Pleasantdale Road, Suite 420
Atlanta, GA 30340-4260
770-447-5083
http://www.aeecenter.org

For general information about the renewable energy industry, contact
Energy Efficiency and Renewable Energy
U.S. Department of Energy
Mail Stop EE-1
Washington, DC 20585
877-337-3463

http://www.eere.energy.gov

For more information about renewable energy and careers, contact
National Renewable Energy Laboratory
1617 Cole Boulevard
Golden, CO 80401-3305
303-275-3000
http://www.nrel.gov

For information on green construction, contact
U.S. Green Building Council
2101 L Street, NW, Suite 500
Washington, DC 20037-1599
http://www.usgbc.org

Growth in the hydropower industry will be limited by the fact that most potential sites for hydropower projects have already been tapped.

Bioenergy is experiencing steady growth, with good employment opportunities for chemists, engineers, and other agricultural scientists.

Employment opportunities in geothermal energy are greatest in the West for the direct use, or drilling, of geothermal energy, and in the Midwest for geothermal heat pumps.

The U.S. Department of Energy reports that advanced water power—such as ocean, river, and tidal currents—is also beginning to be studied as a source of renewable energy.

Teachers, Environmental Science

What Environmental Science Teachers Do

Teachers instruct students of all ages. They develop teaching outlines and lesson plans. They give lectures, lead discussions and activities, keep class attendance records, assign homework, and determine if students are learning. *Environmental science teachers* instruct students about the environment. They teach elementary and secondary students about environmental issues such as global climate change, ozone layer depletion, and endangered species. They teach college-age students about these topics and major environmental fields such as environmental engineering, soil conservation, environmental law, oceanography, wildlife biology, groundwater science, ecology, hazardous waste management, and renewable energy.

Elementary school teachers plan lessons, teach a variety of subjects, and keep records of academic performance, behavior, and attendance for each student. They teach environmental science as part of general science classes or in those that focus specifically on the environment. Elementary school is usually defined as kindergarten through the sixth grade.

Secondary school teachers instruct junior and senior high school students (grades seven through 12). They usually specialize in a certain subject, such as environmental science, biology, ecology, or chemistry, or they may teach several subjects. In addition to classroom instruction, they plan lessons, prepare tests, grade papers, complete report cards, meet with parents, and supervise other activities. They often meet individually with

EXPLORING

- Read books and magazines about teaching.
- Learn as much as you can about environmental issues.
- The requirements of a teacher go far beyond the classroom, so ask to spend some time with one of your teachers after school, and ask to look at lecture notes and record-keeping procedures.
- Volunteer for a peer tutoring program. Other opportunities that will give you teaching experience include coaching an athletic team at the YMCA/YWCA, counseling at a summer camp, teaching a nature course at a community center, or assisting with a community theater production.
- Talk to your teachers about their careers and college experiences.

students to discuss homework assignments, or academic or personal problems. Secondary school teachers have many responsibilities outside of the classroom, as well. They keep grade and attendance records. They prepare lesson plans, exams, and homework assignments. In between classes, they oversee study halls and lunchroom activities. They attend school meetings or meet with parents and students. They may supervise extracurricular activities like sports teams, the school newspaper, or the environmental science club.

College and university faculty instruct students at two-year and four-year colleges and universities. *College environmental science professors* have three main responsibilities: teaching, service, and research. Teaching is the most important. Professors give lectures, lead discussions, give exams, and assign textbook reading and term papers. They may spend fewer than 16 hours a week in the classroom, but they spend many hours preparing lectures and lesson plans, grading papers and exams, and preparing grade reports. They also meet with students individually outside of the classroom to guide them in the course and keep them updated about their progress. All college professors provide important services to their department, college, or profession. Many college professors edit technical journals, review research and scholarship, and head committees about their field of expertise. College professors also serve on committees that determine what classes are offered or make decisions about what methods are used to teach students. Many environmental science professors conduct research in their field of study and publish the results in textbooks and journals.

Tips for Success

To be a successful environmental science teacher, you should

- care deeply about protecting the environment
- be good at educating people about environmental topics and issues
- have excellent communication skills
- have strong leadership abilities
- be a good listener
- have compassion and a genuine interest in your students
- be enthusiastic
- be willing to continue to learn throughout your career

Education and Training

During your middle- and high-school years, you should concentrate on a college preparatory program and focus on learning as much as you can about the environment. When you finish your undergraduate degree and enter a master's program, you will probably be required to work as a teaching assistant.

Elementary and secondary school teachers must have at least a bachelor's degree in an approved teacher training program. Many colleges and universities offer these programs in their education departments. You must take courses in environmental science, as well as a number of education courses covering teaching techniques and related subjects. You must also spend several months as a student teacher under the

DID YOU KNOW?

There are more than 4,500 colleges and universities in the United States. These schools have a chance to make a big environmental impact by conserving water, protecting natural habitats, creating energy efficiency programs, developing good recycling programs, and creating a wide variety of environmental classes for students. In 2008, the National Wildlife Federation partnered with Princeton Survey Research Associates International to conduct a survey of nearly 1,100 colleges and universities to determine which had the best environmental practices. It found that Willamette University in Salem, Oregon, had the best sustainability activities on its campus. Other top schools included the following:

- Georgia Institute of Technology
- Michigan State University
- University of Arizona
- University of North Carolina at Chapel Hill
- Cascadia Community College

Visit http://www.nwf.org/campusEcology/pdfs/FactSheet_FINAL.pdf for more information on the survey.

Source: *America's Campuses in 2008: Leading the Way to a Greener Future*

supervision of an experienced teacher. When you finish the program, you receive certification as a secondary school teacher. Many teachers go on to earn master's degrees in education.

To teach in a four-year college or university, you must have at least a master's degree. With a master's degree you can become an instructor. You will need a doctorate for a job as an assistant professor, which is the entry-level job title for college faculty. Faculty members usually spend no more than six years as assistant professors. During this time, the college will decide whether to grant you tenure, which is a type of job security, and promote you to associate professor.

Earnings

The U.S. Department of Labor (DOL) reports the following salary ranges for teachers by grade level in 2008: elementary,

FOR MORE INFO

To read about the issues affecting college professors, contact
American Association of University Professors
1133 Nineteenth Street, NW, Suite 200
Washington, DC 20036-3655
202-737-5900
aaup@aaup.org
http://www.aaup.org

To read about the issues affecting teachers, contact the following organization:
American Federation of Teachers
555 New Jersey Avenue, NW
Washington, DC 20001-2029
202-879-4400
http://www.aft.org

For information about opportunities at the college level, contact
Association of Environmental Engineering & Science Professors
2303 Naples Court
Champaign IL 61822-3510
http://www.aeesp.org

$33,000 to $78,000 or more; middle, $34,000 to $78,000 or more; and secondary, $34,000 to $81,000 or more.

The mean annual wage for college environmental science teachers was $65,130 in 2008, according to the DOL. Salaries ranged from less than $31,000 to more than $126,000.

Outlook

Employment opportunities for elementary and secondary teachers are expected to be good during the next decade. The U.S. Department of Labor says that science and math teachers will be in especially strong demand.

Employment for college teachers should be strong. College enrollment is projected to grow due to an increased number of 18- to 24-year-olds and because more adults are returning to college to continue their education. There will be strong competition for top positions—especially at four-year universities.

Opportunities will be best for teachers with advanced degrees who have the ability to speak and teach in a foreign language such as Spanish or Mandarin (a Chinese dialect).

Glossary

accredited approved as meeting established standards for providing good training and education; this approval is usually given by an independent organization of professionals

annual salary the money an individual earns for an entire year of work

apprentice a person who is learning a trade by working under the supervision of a skilled worker; apprentices often receive classroom instruction in addition to their supervised practical experience

associate's degree an academic rank or title granted by a community or junior college or similar institution to graduates of a two-year program of education beyond high school

bachelor's degree an academic rank or title given to a person who has completed a four-year program of study at a college or university; also called an **undergraduate degree** or **baccalaureate**

career an occupation for which a worker receives training and has an opportunity for advancement

certified approved as meeting established requirements for skill, knowledge, and experience in a particular field; people are certified by an organization of professionals in their field

college a higher education institution that is above the high school level

community college a public or private two-year college attended by students who do not usually live at the college; graduates of a community college receive an associate's degree and may transfer to a four-year college or university to complete a bachelor's degree

diploma a certificate or document given by a school to show that a person has completed a course or has graduated from the school

distance education a type of educational program that allows students to take classes and complete their education by mail or the Internet

doctorate   the highest academic rank or title granted by a graduate school to a person who has completed a two- to three-year program after having received a master's degree

fellowship   a financial award given for research projects or dissertation assistance; fellowships are commonly offered at the graduate, postgraduate, or doctoral levels

freelancer   a worker who is not a regular employee of a company; they work for themselves and do not receive a regular paycheck

fringe benefit   a payment or benefit to an employee in addition to regular wages or salary; examples of fringe benefits include a pension, a paid vacation, and health or life insurance

graduate school   a school that people may attend after they have received their bachelor's degree; people who complete an educational program at a graduate school earn a master's degree or a doctorate

intern   an advanced student (usually one with at least some college training) in a professional field who is employed in a job that is intended to provide supervised practical experience for the student

internship   1. the position or job of an intern; 2. the period of time when a person is an intern

junior college   a two-year college that offers courses like those in the first half of a four-year college program; graduates of a junior college usually receive an associate's degree and may transfer to a four-year college or university to complete a bachelor's degree

liberal arts   the subjects covered by college courses that develop broad general knowledge rather than specific occupational skills; the liberal arts are often considered to include philosophy, literature and the arts, history, language, and some courses in the social sciences and natural sciences

major   (in college) the academic field in which a student specializes and receives a degree

master's degree   an academic rank or title granted by a graduate school to a person who has completed a one- or two-year program after having received a bachelor's degree

medical degree   a degree awarded to an individual who has completed four years of training at a medical school

medical school   a school that students attend in order to become a physician; people who complete an educational program at a medical school earn either a doctor of medicine (MD) or osteopathic medicine (DO) degree

pension   an amount of money paid regularly by an employer to a former employee after he or she retires from working

scholarship   a gift of money to a student to help the student pay for further education

social studies   courses of study (such as civics, geography, and history) that deal with how human societies work

starting salary   salary paid to a newly hired employee; the starting salary is usually a smaller amount than is paid to a more experienced worker

technical college   a private or public college offering two- or four-year programs in technical subjects; technical colleges offer courses in both general and technical subjects and award associate's degrees and bachelor's degrees

undergraduate   a student at a college or university who has not yet received a degree

undergraduate degree   see **bachelor's degree**

union   an organization whose members are workers in a particular industry or company; the union works to gain better wages, benefits, and working conditions for its members; also called a **labor union** or **trade union**

vocational school   a public or private school that offers training in one or more skills or trades

wage   money that is paid in return for work done, especially money paid on the basis of the number of hours or days worked

Browse and Learn More

Books

Arthus-Bertrand, Yann. *The Future of the Earth: An Introduction to Sustainable Development for Young Readers.* New York: Harry N. Abrams, 2004.

Brewer, Richard. *Conservancy: The Land Trust Movement in America.* Lebanon, N.H.: University Press of New England, 2004.

Challen, Paul C. *Environmental Disaster Alert!* New York: Crabtree Publishing Company, 2004.

Claybourne, Anna, Gillian Doherty, and Rebecca Treays. *Encyclopedia of Planet Earth.* Tulsa, Okla.: Usborne Publishing, 2000.

Cutler, Catherine, Tony Russell, and Martin Walters. *The Illustrated Encyclopedia of Trees of the World.* London, U.K.: Lorenz Books, 2007.

David, Laurie, and Cambria Gordon. *Down-to-Earth Guide to Global Warming.* New York: Scholastic, 2007.

Donald, Rhonda Lucas. *Air Pollution.* New York: Children's Press, 2002.

———. *Endangered Animals.* New York: Children's Press, 2002.

———. *The Ozone Layer.* New York: Children's Press, 2002.

———. *Recycling.* New York: Children's Press, 2002.

———. *Water Pollution.* New York: Children's Press, 2002.

Edelfelt, Roy, and Alan Reiman. *Careers in Education.* 4th ed. New York: McGraw-Hill, 2003.

Fine, Janet. *Opportunities in Teaching Careers.* New York: McGraw-Hill, 2005.

Fletcher, Susan R., Claudia Copeland, Linda Luther, and James E. McCarthy. *Environmental Laws: Summaries of Major Statutes Administered by the Environmental Protection Agency.* Hauppauge, N.Y.: Nova Science Publishers, 2008.

Heitzmann, William Ray. *Opportunities in Marine Science and Maritime Careers.* New York: McGraw-Hill, 2006.

Hunter, Malcolm L., David Lindenmayer, and Aram Calhoun. *Saving the Earth as a Career: Advice on Becoming a Conservation Professional.* Hoboken, N.J.: Wiley-Blackwell, 2007.

Huntrods, David. *For the Love of Scuba.* New York: Weigl Publishers Inc., 2006.

Jefferis, David. *Green Power: Eco-Energy Without Pollution.* New York: Crabtree Publishing Company, 2006.

Kellert, Stephen, and Matthew Black. *The Encyclopedia of the Environment.* New York: Franklin Watts, 1999.

McAlary, Florence, and Judith Love Cohen. *You Can Be a Woman Marine Biologist.* Rev. ed. Marina del Rey, Calif.: Cascade Pass, Inc., 2001.

McDilda, Diane Gow. *365 Ways to Live Green: Your Everyday Guide to Saving the Environment.* Cincinnati, Ohio: Adams Media, 2008.

McGavin, George C. *Endangered: Wildlife on the Brink of Extinction.* Richmond Hill, O.N.: Firefly Books, 2006.

McGhee, Karen, and George McKay. *National Geographic Encyclopedia of Animals.* Washington, D.C.: National Geographic Children's Books, 2006.

McKay, George, ed. *The Encyclopedia of Animals: A Complete Visual Guide.* Berkeley, Calif.: University of California Press, 2004.

McMillan, Beverly, and John A. Musick. *Oceans.* New York: Simon & Schuster Children's Publishing, 2007.

McNamee, Gregory. *Careers in Renewable Energy: Get a Green Energy Job.* Masonville, Colo.: PixyJack Press, 2008.

Morgan, Sally. *From Windmills to Hydrogen Fuel Cells: Discovering Alternative Energy.* Portsmouth, N.H.: Heinemann, 2007.

Needham, Bobbe. *Ecology Crafts for Kids: 50 Great Ways to Make Friends with Planet Earth.* New York: Sterling Publishing, 1998.

Newkirk, Ingrid. *50 Awesome Ways Kids Can Help Animals: Fun and Easy Ways to Be a Kind Kid.* Rev. ed. Boston: Grand Central Publishing, 2006.

Peterson's. *Peterson's Summer Opportunities for Kids & Teenagers.* 26th ed. Lawrenceville, N.J.: Peterson's, 2008.

Rodd, Tony, and Jennifer Stackhouse. *Trees: A Visual Guide.* Berkeley, Calif.: University of California Press, 2008.

Rushforth, Keith, and Charles Hollis. *National Geographic Field Guide to Trees of North America.* Washington, D.C.: National Geographic Books, 2006.

University of California Press. *The Atlas of Endangered Species.* Berkeley, Calif.: University of California Press, 2008.

Williams, Linda. *Earth Sciences Demystified.* New York: McGraw-Hill Professional, 2004.

Periodicals

Friends of the Earth Newsmagazine
http://www.foe.org

Journal of Environmental Health
http://www.neha.org/JEH

Journal of Environmental Quality
https://www.agronomy.org/publications/jeq

Journal of Natural Resources and Life Sciences Education
http://www.jnrlse.org

LAND&People
http://www.tpl.org

National Geographic Explorer
http://magma.nationalgeographic.com/ngexplorer

National Geographic Kids
http://kids.nationalgeographic.com/kids

National Parks
http://www.npca.org

National Wildlife
http://www.nwf.org/News-and-Magazines/National-Wildlife.aspx

Nature Conservancy
http://www.nature.org/magazine

Ranger Rick
http://www.nwf.org

Recycling Today
http://www.recyclingtoday.com

Resource Recycling
http://www.resource-recycling.com

Sierra
http://www.sierraclub.org/sierra

Time for Kids
http://www.timeforkids.com/TFK

Web Sites

About.com: Environmental Issues
http://environment.about.com

Acid Rain
http://www.epa.gov/acidrain

American Camping Association: Find a Camp
http://find.acacamps.org/finding_a_camp.php

American Federation of Teachers: Becoming a Teacher
http://www.aft.org/tools4teachers/career/becoming.htm

American Forests: How to Plant a Tree
http://www.americanforests.org/planttrees/howto.php

American Library Association: Great Web Sites for Kids
http://www.ala.org/greatsites

Animal Corner
http://www.animalcorner.co.uk

Animal Diversity Web
http://animaldiversity.ummz.umich.edu

Animal Fact Guide
http://www.animalfactguide.com

Animaland
http://www2.aspca.org/site/PageServer?pagename=kids_home

Backyard Conservation
http://www.nrcs.usda.gov/feature/backyard

Backyard Nature
http://www.backyardnature.net

BBC Science & Nature
http://www.bbc.co.uk/nature

Canon Envirothon
http://www.envirothon.org

CanopyMeg.com
http://www.canopymeg.com

Careers in Aquatic and Marine Science
http://www.aqua.org/downloads/pdf/Marine_Science_Careers.pdf

Careers in Forestry & Natural Resources
http://www.forestrycareers.org

Careers in Oceanography, Marine Science, and Marine Biology
http://ocean.peterbrueggeman.com/career.html

EcoKids
http://www.ecokids.ca

Environmental Education for Kids!
http://www.dnr.state.wi.us/eek

Environmental Protection Agency
http://www.epa.gov/epawaste/education/teens.htm

Exploratorium
http://www.exploratorium.edu

Exploring Nature Educational Resource
http://www.exploringnature.org

The Goldman Environmental Prize
http://www.goldmanprize.org

The Green Squad
http://www.nrdc.org/greensquad

Greenhouse Effect
http://epa.gov/climatechange/kids/greenhouse.html

Ground Water Adventurers
http://www.groundwateradventurers.org

Insectclopedia
http://www.insectclopedia.com

The Jane Goodall Institute
http://www.janegoodall.org

Kids For a Clean Environment
http://www.kidsface.org

Kids' Planet
http://www.kidsplanet.org

KidsCamps.com
http://www.kidscamps.com

Magic Porthole
http://www.magicporthole.org

MarineBio
http://marinebio.org

National Audubon Society: Just For Kids
http://www.audubon.org/educate/kids

National Geographic Kids
http://kids.nationalgeographic.com

National Park Service: Explore Nature
http://www.nature.nps.gov

National Park Service: Interpretation and Education
http://www.nps.gov/learn

National Recycling Coalition: Where and How to Recycle
http://www.nrc-recycle.org/consumers.aspx

National Renewable Energy Laboratory: Learning About Renewable Energy
http://www.nrel.gov/learning

National Wildlife Federation: Kids & Families
http://www.nwf.org/kids

The Nature Conservancy
http://www.nature.org

Oakland Zoo: Animals
http://www.oaklandzoo.org/animals

PBS: American Field Guide
http://www.pbs.org/americanfieldguide

Planting Science.org
http://www.plantingscience.org

Preparing for a Wildlife Career
http://nationalzoo.si.edu/Education/WildlifeCareers

Recycle City
http://www.epa.gov/recyclecity

Sea Grant Marine Careers
http://www.marinecareers.net

Seaworld: Animals
http://www.seaworld.org

Sierra Club
http://www.sierraclub.org

Underground Adventure
http://www.fieldmuseum.org/undergroundadventure

U.S. Fish & Wildlife Service Students' Page
http://www.fws.gov/educators/students.html

World Wildlife Fund
http://www.worldwildlife.org

Yahoo!: Kids: Animals
http://kids.yahoo.com/animals

Index